D1435480

THE BLOOD OF THE CROSS

THE BLOOD OF
THE CROSS

By

ANDREW MURRAY, D.D.

A Continuation of
"The Power of the Blood of Jesus"

MARSHALL, MORGAN & SCOTT, LTD.
LONDON AND EDINBURGH

First Edition, October 1935

**Printed and made in Great Britain by
Hunt, Barnard & Co., Ltd., London and Aylesbury.**

PREFACE

IN his preface to the Dutch Edition of this volume, the late
Rev. Andrew Murray, M.A., D.D., tells us that it was on a
journey to Europe that his mind was directed definitely to
the consideration of the " power of the blood of Jesus."
That phrase gripped him and seemed to keep demanding from
him, " What does the power of the blood really mean ? "
He says, " My consideration of this question, and my meditation upon the Scriptures to find an answer to it was made a
great blessing to me." On his return to South Africa, he
took up this subject for consideration during Passion
week in his congregation in Wellington. Fifteen addresses
were delivered on that occasion, then five at a later date.
The substance of the first ten of these discourses has already
been published in a companion volume, *The Power of the
Blood of Jesus ;* the remaining ten are now sent forth under
this title, *The Blood of the Cross.*

He published them, he says, " because I am deeply convinced that we Christians can never know too much about
the truths which the blood proclaims. There can be no
freedom of approach to God, nor fellowship with Him,
apart from a truly vital and powerful experience of the
efficacy of the blood of Christ. Its efficacy is a hidden,
spiritual, divine reality, and therefore can be experienced
only in a heart that is humbly and entirely submitted to the
guidance of the Spirit of God. And just in proportion as
we have an insight into the disposition that inspired Christ
to shed His blood, shall we understand and experience what
that power is which can produce that disposition in us.

" Reconciliation and deliverance from guilt will become
the blessed entrance for us into a life in which the blood—
as it was translated into heaven and abides there—will be
truly the power of a divine abiding life in us.

" It is not without hesitancy that I publish these
meditations. There is always the danger, when one attempts
to explain divine mysteries in human words, of leading souls
away from the one thing that can bring blessing to them,

viz., waiting on God for His Spirit to reveal these truths. I have endeavoured to remember that just as the blood is the deepest mystery of redemption, so its power can be experienced only in a disposition akin to that of Him who shed it.

" I cherish the hope that, for those who read these addresses with that disposition, they may be a help and blessing to them, and that they may long be kept engaged in the consideration from every standpoint of what is in truth the centre of God's wondrous counsel of redemption. It is my prayer that the Lord our God may lead all His people, and me also, ever deeper into the blessed experience of a heart and walk in which the blood manifests its power, and into an intercourse with God in the liberty and intimacy which the blood can bring about. May He cause us to experience and manifest what it means to say that we have ' washed our garments and made them white in the blood of the Lamb.' So may it be."

WM. M. DOUGLAS.

Middelburg,
    Union of South Africa.

CONTENTS

CHAPTER I

The Spirit and the Blood

" There are three that bear witness on earth, the Spirit, and the water, and the blood, and these agree in one "—1 John v. 8.

(A Whitsuntide Message)

IN our consideration of the blood of Christ and the glorious things which it accomplishes in us, an objection may arise that it is difficult for us to enjoy these blessings, because we do not clearly understand what those effects are or how the blood accomplishes them. Or even if we do, in some measure, understand, it is not possible for us always to experience its power, because we cannot always actively co-operate with it. Such difficulties arise because we do not remember that God has provided that the blood, as a vital power, automatically and ceaselessly carries on towards perfection its work within us. He had so inseparably bound together the Holy Spirit and the blood that we may rely on Him to make ceaselessly efficacious, in us, through the Spirit, the blessed power of the blood.

This is the thought expressed in our text. The Apostle had in the previous verses (4 and 5) spoken about faith in Jesus, and then he directs attention to the testimony on which that faith rests (vi. 8–11). He mentions three witnesses :

The Water. This refers to an outward and human act, commanded by God to be observed by those who, turning from their sins, presented themselves to Him in Baptism.

The Blood. In this we see what God has done to bring about a real and living cleansing.

Then there is the Spirit, by whom the witness of both the others is confirmed.

In this chapter we shall confine our attention to the truth that the united witness of the Spirit and the blood is the foundation of our faith.

Let us notice the unbroken union of these Witnesses:

    I. In the Work of Redemption.

    II. In our Personal Experience.

I. The union of the Spirit and the Blood in the Work of Redemption.

i. What first demands our attention here is, that it is through the Spirit alone that the blood has its efficacy and power. We read in the epistle to the Hebrews (ix. 14): " How much more shall the blood of Christ, who through the eternal Spirit offered Himself without spot to God, purge your conscience from dead works to serve the living God." The blood possesses its power to cleanse and to make us fit to serve the living God by the Eternal Spirit, who was in our Lord when He shed His blood. This does not mean merely that the Holy Spirit was in the Lord Jesus and bestowed on His person and His blood a divine worth. It is much more than that—it indicates that the shedding of His blood was brought about by the Eternal Spirit, and that the Spirit lived and worked in that blood, so that when it was shed it could not decay as a dead thing, but as a living reality it could be taken up to heaven, to exercise its divine power from thence.

It is expressly for this reason that the Spirit is here called " the Eternal Spirit." " Eternal " is one of the words of Scripture which everyone thinks he understands ; but there are few who realize what a deep and glorious meaning it has. It is supposed that " Eternal " is something that always continues, something that has no end. This explanation is a merely negative one and tells us only what " Eternal " is not, but it teaches us nothing about its nature and being. Everything that exists in time has a beginning and is subject to the law of increase and decrease, of becoming and decaying. What is eternal has no beginning and knows no change or weakening, because it has in itself a life that is independent of time. In what is eternal there is no past which has already disappeared and is lost, and there is no future not yet possessed. It is always a glorious and endless present.

Now, when Scripture speaks of " eternal " life, " eternal " redemption, " eternal " joy, it means much more than to say, merely they will have no end. By that word we are taught that he who has a share in eternal blessedness possesses something in which the power of an endless life is at work ; something in which there can be no change, nor can it suffer any diminution, and which therefore we may always enjoy in the fullness of its life—bestowing blessing.

The object of Scripture in using that word is to teach us that if our faith lays hold on what is eternal, it will manifest itself in us as a power superior to all the changeableness of our mind or feelings, with a youth which never grows old, and with a freshness which does not for a moment wither.

From this Scripture we are taught something also about the blood of Jesus—" Who through the eternal Spirit offered Himself without spot to God." Not only had the act of shedding His blood an eternally availing worth ; the blood itself has Spirit and life in it, and is always efficacious by the power of an eternal life. This is why the Epistle to the Hebrews lays much emphasis on the work of Christ as being once for all, and eternal. Notice the expression in chapter vii. 17—He is " a priest for ever after the order of Melchizedek." " After the power of an eternal life " (verse 16). He has an " unchanging priesthood." " Wherefore He is able also to save to the uttermost them that come unto God by Him, seeing He ever liveth to make intercession for them " (verses 24, 25). He is " the Son who is consecrated for evermore " (verse 28). Further on we read (chapter ix. 12) : " By His own blood He entered in once into the holy place, having obtained eternal redemption for us ; " and in x. 14 : " By one offering He hath perfected for ever them that are sanctified." It speaks also of " the blood of the everlasting covenant." By the eternal Spirit the blood has obtained an eternal, ever-availing, ever-fresh, independent, imperishable power of life.

ii. But the correlative is also true. As the blood possesses its power through the Spirit, so the Spirit manifests His full power and works effectively among men only through the blood.

We know that the outpouring of the blood was followed by the outpouring of the Spirit. And we know the reason of this. By sin, a middle wall of partition separated God and man. "The flesh" was the veil that made true union impossible. As long as sin was not atoned for, God by His Spirit could not take up a settled abode in the heart of man. Until the power of the flesh was broken and subdued, the Spirit could not manifest his authority. For this reason there is no mention in the days of the Old Testament of an outpouring of the Spirit of God, save as a prediction of what should be in the last days. Therefore also our Lord Jesus was not in a position to bestow upon His disciples the Spirit with whom He had been baptised, even though He took them into the closest fellowship with Himself; though He greatly loved them and longed to bless them.

Our Lord had to die before He could baptise with the Holy Spirit. The blood is the life of man; the Spirit is the life of God. Man must sacrifice his sinful life, bear the penalty of his sin, and surrender himself entirely to God before God could dwell in him with His life. What man himself could not do, that the Lord Jesus, the Son of Man, did for him. He shed His blood, He gave His life in entire surrender to the will of God as a satisfaction of the penalty of sin. When that was accomplished, it was possible for Him to receive the Spirit from the Father, that He might pour Him out. The outpouring of the blood rendered possible the outpouring of the Spirit.

This is declared in the Scriptures in such words as these: "The Spirit was not yet given, because Jesus was not yet glorified." And again: "He showed me a pure river of the water of life, clear as crystal, proceeding out of the throne of God, and of the Lamb " (Rev. xxii. 1). It was when the Lamb took possession of the throne with the Father that the Spirit could flow out as a river. In the preaching of John the Baptist these were, also, the two statements he made about Jesus : " Behold the Lamb of God which taketh away the sin of the world," and " This is He who baptiseth with the Holy Spirit."

It was necessary for our High Priest to enter into " the Holiest " with His blood, and, having come out again, to appear before the Throne with that blood, ere He could bestow the Spirit from the Throne, as the seal that His work in the Holiest had wrought out a perfect reconciliation. The blood and the Spirit are inseparable, for only through the blood can the Spirit dwell in man.

iii. In the execution of the work of Redemption also, the activities of the blood and the Spirit are inseparably connected.

This is why we find, in Scripture, that what in one place is ascribed to the Spirit, is in another place ascribed to the blood, and the work of sanctification is ascribed to both the blood and the Spirit. Life also is ascribed to both. Our Lord said : " He that eateth My flesh and drinketh My blood hath everlasting life," adding afterwards " It is the Spirit that quickeneth, the flesh profiteth nothing " (John vi. 54, 63). We find similar expressions in the epistle to the Ephesians. After having said " Ye . . . are made nigh by the blood of Christ " (ii. 13), a little later Paul declares (verse 18) that " We . . . have access by one Spirit to the Father." So also in the epistle to the Hebrews, the contemning of the blood and of the Spirit is treated as one act. We read of those " who counted the blood of the covenant an unholy thing, and have done despite unto the Spirit of grace " (Heb. x. 20).

We have noticed that the " blood " is a word chosen by

God as a short way of expressing certain thoughts, powers, and dispositions, which are, as it were, included in it. It is not always easy, either in preaching or in personal exercise of faith, to find a perfect expression of these thoughts, powers, and dispositions. But this is what the Holy Spirit undertakes as His work, especially where faith is exercised about the blood; He will explain, and make living, the full and glorious meaning of the word. By enlightening our understanding, He will make clear to us the great thoughts of God which are contained in the words "the blood." Even before the understanding can lay hold of them, He will make their power active in the soul; and where a heart, desiring salvation, is humbly and reverently seeking for the blessings they bring, He will bestow them. And He will not only send the power of the blood *to* the heart, but will so reveal it *in* the heart that the same disposition which inspired Jesus in the shedding of His blood will be awakened in us, as it is written: "They overcame by the blood of the Lamb . . . ; and they loved not their lives even unto the death" (Rev. xii. 11).

It is the great work of the Holy Spirit to glorify Jesus: to make Him glorious in human hearts, by bestowing the blessed experience of His redemption. And because the blood is the central point of redemption, the Holy Spirit will make the blood appear specially glorious *to* us and will glorify it *in* us. We can form some idea of the blood that was shed on earth in connection with the sin offering, but we have little conception of the blood that in "the Holiest" on high speaks and works in the power of eternal life. The Holy Spirit, however, comes with His heavenly, life-giving power to enable us to appropriate that which is eternal, and to make it a real, living, inward experience in us.

Faith in the atoning efficacy of the blood, and in the personality of the Holy Spirit, are two truths which always are both denied when the church turns aside to error, while both of them are held fast by the true Church of God. Where the blood is honoured, preached, and believed in as the power of full redemption, there the way is opened for the fullness of the Spirit's blessing. And in proportion as the Holy Spirit truly works in the hearts of men, He always leads them to glory in the blood of the Lamb. "And I beheld, and lo, in the midst of the throne . . . stood a Lamb as it had been slain, having . . . seven eyes which are the seven spirits of God" (Rev. v. 6). The blood and the Spirit proceed together from the Lamb, and together they bear witness to Him alone.

II. The union of the Blood and the Spirit in our Personal Experience.

We lay emphasis on this to show what rich comfort and blessing this truth contains for us. We must once again notice the two sides of this truth : the blood exercises its full efficacy through the Spirit; and the Spirit manifests His full power through the blood.

i. The blood exercises its full power through the Spirit. We have here a glorious answer to the questions that at once arise in the minds of seekers after salvation. I have no doubt that by what has been written on the power of the blood of Jesus—about the rich, full blessing which is found in that blood—that questions have arisen such as :—

"How is it that the blood is not more efficacious in my life ? "

"How can I experience its full power ? "

"Is there any hope for a person so weak as I am, and one who understands so little, to expect that fullness of blessing ? "

Listen to the answer, all you who heartily and sincerely long for it ! The Holy Spirit dwells within you, and it is His office to glorify the Lamb, and the blood of the Lamb. The Spirit and the blood bear witness together. The mistake we make is in thinking of the blood as if it alone bare witness. We think of the shedding of the blood as an event that occurred nineteen hundred years since, on which we are to look back, and by the exercise of faith to represent it as present and real—and, as our faith is always weak, we feel that we cannot do this as it ought to be done. As a result of this mistaken idea, we have no powerful experience of what the blood can do.

This weakness of faith arises, in the case of honest hearts, from imperfect conceptions concerning the power of the blood. If I regard the blood, not as something which lies inactive and must be aroused to activity by my faith, but as an almighty, eternal power which is always active, then my faith becomes, for the first time, a true faith. Then I shall understand that my weakness cannot interfere with the power of the blood. I have simply to honour the blood by exalted ideas of its power to overcome every hindrance. The blood will manifest its power in me, because the eternal Spirit of God always works *with* it and *in* it.

Was it not through the Eternal Spirit that, when Jesus died, His blood had power to conquer sin and death, so that Jesus was " brought again from the dead by the blood of the everlasting covenant " (Heb. xiii. 20) ?

Was it not through the Eternal Spirit that the blood penetrated the regions of holy light and life to heaven itself and bears there its peculiar relationship to God the Father, and to Jesus the Mediator ?

Is it not through the Eternal Spirit that the blood ever continues to manifest its power on the innumerable multitude which is being gathered together ?

Is it not the Eternal Spirit who dwells in me as a child of God, on whom I may rely to make the blood of Jesus glorious in me also ? Thank God, it is so. I have no need to fear. In the childlike heart, conscious of its weakness, and wholly surrendered to the Lamb of God in order to experience the power of His blood, the Holy Spirit will do His work. We may confidently rely upon the Spirit to reveal in us the omnipotent effects of the blood.

But there is another difficulty. When we recognise

[16]

that the blood is omnipotent in its effects, then we would limit the continuance of its activities to the period of our own active co-operation with it. You imagine that, so long as you can *think* about it, and your faith is actively engaged with it, the blood will manifest its power in you. But there is a very large part of your life during which you must be engaged with earthly business, and you do not believe that, during these hours, the blood can continue its active work quite undisturbed. And yet it is so. If you have the necessary faith, if you definitely commit yourself to the sanctifying power of the blood for those hours during which you cannot be thinking about it, then you can be sure that your soul may continue, undisturbed, under the blessed activities of the blood. That is the meaning, the comfort, of what we said about the word " eternal " and the " eternal redemption " which the blood has purchased. Eternal is that in which " the power of an imperishable life " works ceaselessly every moment. Through the eternal Spirit, the precious blood possesses this ceaselessly efficacious power of eternal life : the soul may, with even greater confidence, entrust itself to Him for every hour of business engagements, or of special rush and bustle ; for the activity of the blood will continue without hindrance. Just as a fountain which is supplied by or from an abundant store of water streams out day and night with a cleansing and refreshing flow, so the blessed streams of this fountain of life will flow over and through the soul that dares to expect it from her Lord.

And just as the Holy Spirit is the life-power of these omnipotent and ever-flowing streams of the blessed efficacy of the blood, so it is He also who prepares us, and makes it possible for us to recognise and receive these streams by faith.

Spiritual things must be spiritually discerned. Our human thought cannot apprehend the mysteries of the " the Holiest " in heaven. This is especially true concerning the unspeakable glory of the holy blood in heaven. Let us with deep reverence entrust ourselves to the teaching of the Spirit, waiting on Him in holy stillness and awe that He may witness with, and of, the blood.

As often as we longingly pray for the holy power of the blood, let us with great tenderness open our hearts to the influences of the Spirit; the Spirit and the blood always bear witness together. Through the eternal Spirit the full power of the blood will be exercised in us.

There is another glorious side to this truth :—

ii. The Spirit attains His full power in us, through the blood. Just as the outpouring of the Spirit followed the outpouring of the blood and its translation into heaven, so it is also in the heart. In proportion as the blood obtains a place in the heart, and is honoured there, so the Spirit is free to carry on His work.

At Ascensiontide we remember the Passion and resurrection of our Lord, and look forward to Pentecost [1] and the days of prayer during which we wait on the Lord that we may be filled by His Spirit.

Each year we are thus reminded that it is the will of Him " Who baptises with the Holy Spirit," that His disciples should be filled with the Spirit. " Full of the Holy Spirit " is not set forth in Scripture as the privilege of a particular time, or of a certain people, but is plainly represented as the privilege of every believer who surrenders himself to live wholly for, and in fellowship with, Jesus. Whitsuntide is not just a remembrance of something that once happened and then passed away, but it is the celebration of the opening of a fountain which ever flows, and it is the promise of that which is always the right, and the characteristic, of those who belong to the Lord. We ought to be, and we must be, filled with the Holy Spirit.

[1] *Note by the Translator :*—The Dutch Reformed Church in South Africa has for many years observed the ten days between Ascension and Whitsunday as days of continuous and united prayer. It is impossible to tell how great and abiding has been the blessing of God on these gatherings.

The lesson which the Word of God has taught us, shows the preparation necessary for the baptism of the Spirit. For the first disciples, as well as for the Lord Jesus, the path to Whitsuntide ran by Golgotha. The outpouring of the Spirit is inseparably bound up with the previous outpouring of the blood. With us also it is a new and deeper experience of what the blood can accomplish, that will lead us to the full blessing of Whitsuntide.

If you long for this blessing, consider, I beseech you, the immovable foundation on which it rests. Take such a word as that from John : " The blood of Jesus Christ His Son cleanseth us from all sin " (1 John i. 7). The cleansed vessel can be filled. Come with all the sins of which you are conscious, and ask the Lamb to cleanse you in His blood. Receive that word with a perfect faith, with a faith that rejoices over all feeling and experience—" It has taken place for me." Faith acts as possessing what it does not feel ; it knows how, now, in the spirit, to take possession of that which only later on will be realised in the soul, and in the body.

Walking in the light, you have a right to say, with perfect liberty, " The blood of Jesus Christ cleanseth me from all sin." Rely on your Great High Priest to manifest in your heart also, by His Spirit, the heavenly wonder-working power which His blood has exercised for cleansing in " the Holiest." Rely on the blood of the Lamb which destroyed the authority and effect of sin before God, in heaven, to destroy it also in your heart. And let your song of joy, by faith, be " Unto Him who cleansed me in His own blood be the glory and the power," and reckon on receiving the fullness of the Spirit. It is by the Spirit that the blood was offered up. It is by the Spirit that the blood has had its power, and is still efficacious, in your heart. It is by the Spirit that your heart, through the blood, has been made a temple of God. Reckon, with full assurance of faith, that a heart which is, through Him, " by blood made clean," is prepared, as a temple, to be filled with the glory of God. Reckon on the fullness of the Spirit as your portion.

Oh, the blessedness of a heart " by blood made clean," and filled with the Spirit! Full of joy, and full of love; full of faith, and full of praise; full of zeal, and full of power—for the work of the Lord. By the blood and the Spirit of the Lamb that heart is a temple where God dwells, on His throne of grace; where God himself is the light, where God's will is the only law, where the glory of God is all in all. Oh, ye children of God, come and let the precious blood prepare you for being filled with His Spirit, so that the Lamb that was slain for you may have the reward of His labour—labour marked by blood—and He and you together may be satisfied in His love.

CHAPTER II

The Blood-bought Multitude : The Relation of the Blood to Missionary Effort

" And they sung a new song, saying, Thou art worthy to take the book, and to open the seals thereof : for Thou wast slain, and hast redeemed us to God by Thy blood out of every kindred, and tongue, and people, and nation "—Rev. v. 9.

WHEN we lay our gifts for the work of the Lord upon His altar, it should not be done from mere custom, or without serious thought. Every penny that comes into His treasury has a value corresponding to the intention with which it is offered to Him ; only true love to Him and His work transforms our gifts into spiritual offerings. It would be well for us to learn what God thinks and says about missionary work if we are to think and act according to His will.

The work of the missionary is always a work of faith— faith which is the sure evidence of things man cannot see ; it is guided in everything by what is seen or heard in the unseen world. The outstanding value of missionary work lies in the fact that it is a work of faith. It has always been something beyond mere human comprehension, for mere human wisdom cannot understand it, and the natural man has no love for it. He cannot imagine how it is possible for a raw heathen to be tamed and renewed by nothing save the message of the love of God in Christ.

The men who in all ages have stood at the head of the great missionary undertakings have received from heaven, by the Word and Spirit of God, the light and power needed for their work. It was the eye of faith fixed on Jesus as King that opened their hearts to receive His command and His promise, in which they found both the impulse and the courage for their work.

Our text tells us of a vision of things in " the heavenlies " which sheds the light of eternity upon the work of missions. We hear the song of the redeemed who praise the Lamb that He had redeemed them to God by His blood. And in their song, that which is mentioned as of prime importance after the praise of the Lamb—or rather that is one part of that praise—is the fact that they were gathered together out of " every kindred, and tongue, and nation." This is mentioned in praise of the power which the blood had exercised : there was no kindred, nor nation, which had not its representatives among those redeemed by the blood of the Lamb : there was no division of language or nationality of which the breach had not been healed ; all were united in one spirit of love, and in one body, before the throne.

What else is that vision save a heavenly revelation of the high calling and glorious result of mission work ? Without mission work that vision could not have become fact, nor could that song have been sung. In that song is set forth the divine right of missionary work, and the heavenly supply which empowers it. Every time a friend of missions, or the people of God, hear the notes of that song, they receive a loud call to fresh courage and renewed consecration, and to fresh joy in the glorious work of gathering together the " great multitude which no man can number."

In these chapters on " the power of the blood," we have hitherto fixed our attention chiefly on its effects in the individual soul. It is right that we should now, for once, inquire into the far-reaching extent and wonderfully powerful effects of His blood in the world.

Missionary work will appear in a new light to us when we see in what relationship it stands to the blood that is so precious to us, and we shall be strengthened to serve the missionary cause, if we understand that the power behind it is nothing less than " the power of the blood of Jesus." We shall learn that in order to carry on that work we must ever regard it as a work of faith ; a work which receives its recommendation, not from what is seen on earth, but from what is heard from heaven.

In order to understand this better, let us consider mission work :

I.   In Connection with the Difficulties it has to Encounter on Earth.

II.   In the Light that Falls upon it From Heaven.

I.   The Difficulties the Missionary Cause has to Encounter on Earth.

These have chiefly to do with the field of labour, the labourers, and the fruit of those labours.   We shall consider these difficulties, first of all with an eye on South Africa, and on the reflections upon, or hesitation about, the missionary cause which are sometimes found even among well-meaning people.

i.   The Mission Field.

Just that which provided the great multitude with their glory and joy, is here on earth one of the greatest hindrances to mission work : the separation between peoples and nations.   The judgment upon the sin of Babel—the division of mankind, by confusing their languages—is a real curse, under which mankind sighs.   In the old heathen world, everyone who did not belong to the tribe or clan was reckoned as a natural enemy.   Even among the peoples of Europe, how much hatred and strife exists ; how much contempt and enmity !   The difficulty this creates for the Gospel cannot easily be conceived.

Sometimes the messenger who brought the Gospel belonged to a despised or hostile nation.   It was no small stumbling-block, that in the extension of the Kingdom of Christ, the proud Roman had to receive the Gospel from the despised Jew.   In the history of the introduction of Christianity into Germany, into Holland, and Scotland, it is often recorded that the messengers could obtain no entrance, because they belonged to a hostile people. And even in our own day the reproach of the poor heathen is often directed against the missionary—" your people have taken away the land that belonged to my people ; how can I receive your religion ? " Or he points out so much that is wrong and disgraceful in those belonging to the people from whom the missionary comes, and says " Take your message first to your own people : why do they not receive your Jesus ? "

Then, further, there is the difficulty that lies on the other side. The people to whom the Gospel must be brought are degraded and despised. At all times the worldly-wise people have said that the heathen must be civilised first, for then only would they be capable of receiving the Gospel. When the first German missionary, Ziegenbalg, went to India in 1705, he and his friends were named by a renowned University, " fanatics," " unsent apostles." When toward the end of that century, in 1796, the cause of missions was for the first time considered in the General Assembly of the Church of Scotland, the proposal to take part in the movement was thrown out, because it was, they thought, contrary to nature to send the Gospel to a people, until they became civilised. For many years in Europe the thought that a Bushman or a Hottentot in their degraded state could experience the power of the Gospel, was considered the greatest absurdity. Only a living faith in the revelation given from heaven, that men from every kindred, and tongue, and nation have been redeemed, can supply the courage or power to undertake mission work.

ii. The labourers furnish no fewer difficulties than the field of labour. When, about a hundred years ago, the missionary spirit was awakened again in Europe, and the missionary societies could find but few ministers who had completed their ordinary course of studies who were willing to go out, they were glad to accept men who had a passion for the work, and to send them out, after a short course of training. Much criticism was levelled against the folly of expecting that such labourers could succeed in a work so difficult, if not impossible, to accomplish.

And yet it was men of such imperfect training who became heroes of the Cross, such as Carey—" the sanctified cobbler," as he was called in derision— and John Williams, and others, who are now recognised by the Church of Christ, where she knows and loves mission work, as the benefactors of humanity, and the glory of Christ. When, later on, it was proved that men of learning and higher training were valued in the movement, then it was asked, what need had one who laboured among uncivilised people to be so learned ?—or how could he stoop to the depth wherein the spirit of the degraded heathen lay ? The labourers, as seen and judged by the wisdom of this world, could not be believed to be the instruments by which the kingdom of Satan should be overthrown and the way opened for Jesus to be crowned as Conqueror.

There are many other difficulties which appear as we think of the labourers. What criticisms have there not been in South Africa ? We remember how often it has been said that if Dr. Phillip and the first men of the London Missionary Society had been in closer touch with the farming population of South Africa, who were Christians, and also with the masters who possessed slaves, much of the enmity and condemnation of missionary work might have been avoided. Some of us still remember how at the first Conference at Worcester which God so richly blessed, in 1860, the one thing by which agreement in the spirit of love and joy was almost destroyed, was a criticism by a German brother of our farmers ; and the reply that if the missionary sought to co-operate more with the farmers, interest in the work among the heathen would have increased. At a still later time the same reproach was often heard concerning a number of missionaries, who, from all who knew them, had the highest personal praise given to them—the French missionaries in Basutoland—that more love and fellowship with the Church in the Free State would have helped to win sympathy and support for their Mission.

It is not necessary nor possible to pass judgment here on the amount of truth which may be found in such criticisms; I mention them merely to point out how truly this division between peoples, and languages, and nations, which one day will form part of the glory of the great multitude of the redeemed, is here on earth one of the greatest difficulties in the accomplishment of that work. From our point of view of mission work, it is indeed a work of faith. He who will wait till all the labourers are what he would like them to be, understands little about "a work of faith": he who accepts the word of the Lord Jesus, and builds upon it, thanks God for every witness who makes the Lord known to the heathen, even though the witness be imperfect.

iii. There is still the difficulty arising from the Fruit of Missions.

This includes the more immediate fruit of the work—the converts, and also those who have received the teaching, but have not become real believers.

As to the converts: how often one hears complaints about the imperfection, the lack of trustworthiness, or truth; or neglect of other duties which should characterise the Christian! It is forgotten that a true conversion does not include, at once, full sanctification; that the sanctification found in the old Christian peoples is the fruit of a thousand years' intercourse, under the discipline and training of the Word of God; that the Apostles—as for instance Paul—had to give instructions in his Epistles about lying, and stealing, and adultery, to those whom he addresses as truly regenerated persons, because they had so recently been delivered from heathenism (Eph. iv. 20-28; Col. iii. 1-10). But even among European Christians, and sometimes among truly pious persons, there remains much to be desired in what concerns truth and honour, love and righteousness; and though we may well sorrow over the failures of those recently converted from heathenism, this ought not to lead to condemnation or discouragement. The Word of God and His grace need time to produce these fruits.

Then there is, further, the complaint concerning the influence learning exercises on those who have not been converted. "Knowledge puffs up": they obtain new thoughts about their value as human beings; they become unfit for service. A raw heathen is preferred, it is said, to the taught Kaffir who has been at school. One thinks that the missionary does not sufficiently preach "submission" as a first duty of the coloured people; another gives his judgment that the fault is that the education of the Kaffir is not confined to mere reading and writing. It is desirable that the Bible should be taught, and that the way of salvation should be made plain, but higher education is not for them, and does them only harm. How is it that mission work and social interests seem to be at times in conflict with one another? What the Gospel has done for our forefathers in the awakening of personal worth, of liberty, of progress, it effects also in the coloured people; and out of the fermentation of this yeast more than one difficulty arises.

Truly in the midst of so much which awakens opposition to missions, faith is necessary, if we are to continue to be friends of the movement. Faith does not shut her eyes to the difficulties which exist, nor does she wait till they are removed. The command has been heard by her from the King on the Throne. She had heard the sound of the song of the redeemed, from every kindred and tongue and nation; she has experienced in her own heart the wonderful power of the blood, in the midst of all hesitation and deficiencies she rejoices over every labourer who simply proclaims Jesus, and over every soul who begins to learn, even in weakness, to call upon that name.

II. The Light which Falls from Heaven upon Mission Work.

It is in this that faith finds her power. In the song of the great multitude gathered by missionary activity, we hear that it is the blood of the Lamb by which they were redeemed, to which they owe their participation in salvation. Let us consider how that blood is, in truth, the power of the missionary movement. It is that blood alone that bestows the courage, awakens the love, and provides the weapons, to which missions owe their victory.

i. The blood bestows courage. We may well ask whence came the thought into the hearts of weak men and women, of daring to attempt such a task as attacking the power of Satan, in heathendom, and robbing him of his prey? If the thought had come from the great statesmen, or from the warriors who had conquered the peoples of the heathen world, and intended in this matter also to conquer them; or if it had come from men of learning, who believe in the power of knowledge and civilization, then we might perhaps have understood it. But no, these men were generally the most fierce opponents of the work. The thought was conceived and cherished in the quietness of hidden circles, of those who were of no consideration or influence in the world.

What was it then which gave them the needed courage? It was nothing else than the blood of Christ, and faith in the power of that blood. They saw in the Word of God, that God had " Set forth Christ as a propitiation through faith in his blood "—a propitiation " for the sins of the whole world." They saw that that blood availed for every kindred and tongue and nation. It was granted to them to perceive that the blood had been carried into heaven, and is now set down before the throne, as the ransom for the deliverance of souls for whom it had been lawfully paid. They heard the voice of the Father to the Son " Ask of Me and

I will give thee the heathen for thine inheritance"; they knew that no power of hell could prevent the Lord Jesus from seeing of the travail of His soul and being satisfied. Satan was conquered by that blood and was cast out of heaven; that blood had power to conquer him on earth also and to deliver his prisoners out of his hand. By the sprinkling of that blood in heaven the power of sin was for ever broken, and all that could hinder the outflowing of the love or blessing of God towards the most unworthy was removed, and the way opened for His people through faith and prayer, to obtain heavenly power, so that in their weakness they might perform wondrous things. They knew with certainty that the blood of Jesus Christ, God's Son, was the pledge that men from every people and tongue should bow before Jesus.

ii. The blood that bestowed courage to believe this, awakened also love to act on that belief. We, here on earth, speak of blood relationship as being the strongest which exists; the blood of Jesus awakens the sentiment of a heavenly blood relationship, not only among those who are already cleansed but also for those for whom that blood was shed. The blood of Christ expresses the surrender of love, even to death; it is, therefore, the death of selfishness, and opens the fountain of an eternal love in the heart.

The more deeply the believer lives in the power of the blood of Christ the more clearly he views mankind, even the heathen, in the light of redemption. That the blood has been shed for the most degraded, bestows a value on every man and forms the band of a love which embraces all.

The confidence of faith—that the blood will obtain its recompense out of every tongue and nation—should be followed by a purpose of love. I, who myself owe everything to that blood, must bear witness to it, and make it known to those who have not yet heard of it.

That blood for all—also for me: in that faith the soul obtains a share in its blessing. That blood is for me—

therefore also for all : in that faith, love burns, and sacrifices self to make it known to others. Yes, that blood is the power of mission work, for it is those who live in the full fellowship of that blood, who are driven by the love of Christ to carry the tidings to others of that glorious portion that belongs to them.

The friends of missions have need of nothing less than love with its super-earthly power. It is this love alone, brought down to earth, which is able to embrace the wretched ones, and to persevere when all hope seems lost. There are mission fields where God's servants have laboured for twenty or thirty years without seeing any fruit for their labour, and supporters of Societies in Europe have asked if it did not appear to be God's will not to open a door there, but love of souls enabled them to persevere, and later on a rich and blessed harvest has been reaped.

In spite of all the difficulties among us by which mission work seems at times to be surrounded, the heart that burns with love to Christ refuses to relinquish it. The labourer may be imperfect, and the work evidently gives but a small return at home, and abroad it may appear to the eye of flesh that loss, rather than gain, is the result ; but love is not frightened. Souls which have been redeemed by the blood of Christ are too dear to her, she will wrestle on through all difficulties to save those whom she reckons to be of one blood in the Second Adam. It is the blood, that blood which speaks of the love of the Lamb, that is the power of missionary endeavour.

iii. The blood is at the same time the weapon used by missionaries in the strife.

It is not enough that the believer has courage and love for the work, and power to begin it, and persevere with it. Where can he obtain power to really touch the darkened heart, so as to incline and to move it to forsake the gods of its forefathers ; to receive the teaching of the Cross along with sacrifice of everything that the natural man desires, and listen to the call to a heavenly and spiritual life? That power the missionary movement finds in the blood of the cross.

That blood is the proof of a love that surpasses all understanding. That blood is the pledge of a reconciliation and a pardon just such as the awakened soul needs. That blood brings a peace and a cleansing which breaks the power of sin, and banishes it. The Holy Spirit bears witness along with that blood, as He opens the heart for this love and this redemption. Just as the veil was once rent by that blood, so also now by that blood the thick veil on the most sinful heart is destroyed by that blood. It is by the preaching of the grace of God towards the ungodly, by which in the case of thousands of the most degraded idolators, their hearts have been broken and renewed and have become the temple of God.

The history of missions supplies the most touching proofs of this. Thus we learn that in the beginning of mission work in Greenland the missionaries thought that they must first teach the poor Eskimo about God and His law, about sin and righteousness. They did that for more than twenty years without awakening them out of their deadly carelessness. On a certain evening a brother read to a single heathen who had visited him, a portion of the New Testament which he had translated. It was the story of the agony in Gethsemane. " Read that again " said the man. When he had re-read it, he asked the missionary what it meant. When the missionary began to explain the sufferings and death of God's Son the heathen's heart was broken. He was immediately enabled to believe, and then followed a glorious work. The blood of the cross had won the victory.

It is more than one hundred years since that occurred. But every mission field supplies proof that what the wisdom of this world cannot do, has been done through simple men and women, by their message about the blood of the Lamb. And it is because there are thousands of God's children who heartily believe this, that they will not allow themselves, by any means, to be turned away from their love for the glorious, precious work of missions, by which " the multitude which no man can number " is gathered together, to sing the new song in praise of the Lamb that redeemed them to God by His blood. Beloved Christians, there is one question that presses itself upon all of us who profess to be redeemed by the blood of Jesus. The question is " What is the value of that blood to us ? "

Is it of sufficient value to us to lead us to offer ourselves as a sacrifice to the love which caused it to be shed, and to bear witness to it ? Is it indeed to us the most glorious thing in heaven or on earth, so that we have surrendered everything for it, that that precious blood may have its full authority over the whole earth ? Is it worth so much to us that we long that every creature on earth should know about it, and obtain a share in it ? Is it worth so much to us that mission work by which alone the unnumbered multitude redeemed by that blood can be gathered together to sing the praises of the Lamb, and to satisfy His love—is the blood worth this to us, that in us the missionary movement has true, warm, praying, helpful friends ?

Oh, that it may be so ! In spite of all its deficiencies, mission work is God's work. Already God has done great things through it. In South Africa there are those redeemed out of heathenism who have lived to truly honour our Lord, and who have had testimony borne that they pleased God. Do not, I pray you, allow yourselves to be led astray by the talk of those who judge of it by the eye of the flesh, or in the light of time, and the interests of time.

He who does not love Jesus cannot understand mission work : for he knows nothing about the secret blessing of missions, and the redemption of souls. Mission work is the work of eternity : therefore it is a work of faith. Just as the Lord Jesus Himself was despised when He was upon earth, and not esteemed, yet the glory of God was in Him, so also is it with mission work. God is with it; is in it. Do not allow yourselves to be misled by its outward weakness and deficiencies, to misunderstand it. Live for it; give to it; work for it; speak for it; pray for it. If you are a Christian be also a friend of missions. He who knows the power of the blood in his own heart cannot be anything else than a friend of missions. I pray you, by the blood of the Lamb, by your hope of one day joining in the song of the Lamb, by your hope of being welcomed by the un-numbered multitude as a companion in redemption, live as one of the witnesses of the blood of Jesus. As you live only by the blood, live also only for the blood, and give yourself no rest till all His purchased ones know of His glory.

CHAPTER III

The Blood of the Cross

" (God) having made peace through the blood of His cross, by Him to reconcile all things unto Himself; by Him, whether things in earth or things in heaven " —Col. i. 20.

THE Apostle uses here an expression of deep significance : —" the blood of His cross." We know how greatly he valued the expression "the cross of Christ." It expressed, in a brief phrase, the entire power and blessing of the death of our Lord for our redemption ; the subject of his preaching ; the hope and glory of his life. By the expression here used he shows how, on one side the blood possesses its value from the cross on which it was shed ; and on the other, that it is through the blood that the cross reveals its effect and power. Thus the cross and the blood throw reflected light on one another. In our inquiry into what the Scripture teaches concerning the power of the blood, we shall find it of great importance to consider what this expression has to teach us ; what is meant by the blood, as " the blood of the cross." It will enable us to view from a new standpoint, the truths which we have already discovered in that phrase " the blood."

Let us fix our attention on the following points :—

I. The Disposition of our Lord from Which the Cross Derived its Value.

II. The Power it Has Thus Obtained.

III. The Love Which Bestows Everything on Us.

I. The Disposition from Which the Cross Derived its Power.

We are so accustomed, in speaking about the Cross of Christ, to think only of the work that was done there for us, that we take too little notice of that from which that work derives its value—the inner disposition of our Lord of which the cross was only the outward expression. Scripture does not place in the foreground, as most important, the weighty and bitter sufferings of the Lord, which are often emphasised for the purpose of awakening religious feelings, but the inner disposition of the Lord, which led Him to the cross, and inspired Him while on it—this, Scripture does emphasise. Neither does Scripture direct attention only to the work which the Lord accomplished for us on the cross ; it directs special attention to the work that the cross accomplished in Him, and which through Him must yet be accomplished in us also.

This appears not only from our Lord's words which He spoke from the cross, but from what He said when on three different occasions He had previously told His disciples that they must take up their cross and follow Him. More than once He spoke thus when foretelling His own crucifixion. The thought he wished specially to impress upon them in connection with the cross was that of fellowship with, of conformity to, Him. And that this did not consist in merely outward sufferings and persecutions, but in an inward disposition, appears from what He often added, "deny yourselves and take up the cross." This is what he desires them to do. Our Lord further teaches us, that neither for Him nor for His disciples does the bearing of the Cross begin when a material cross is laid upon the shoulders. No! He carried the Cross all through His life ; what became visible on Golgotha was a manifestation of the disposition which inspired His whole life.

What then did the bearing of the Cross mean for the Lord Jesus ? And what end could it serve for Him ? We know that the evil of sin appears in the change it brought about both in the disposition of man towards God, as well as in that of God towards man. With man it resulted in his fall from God, or enmity against God ; with God it resulted in His turning away from man, or His wrath. In the first we see the terribleness of its tyranny over man; in the second, the terribleness of the guilt of sin, demanding the judgment of God on man.

The Lord Jesus, who came to deliver man from sin as a whole, had to deal with the power of sin as well as with its guilt; first the one, and then the other. For although we separate these two things, for the sake of making truth clear, sin is ever a unity. Therefore we need to understand not only that our Lord by His atonement on the cross removed the guilt of sin, but that this was made possible by the victory He had first won over the power of sin. It is the glory of the cross that it was the divine means by which both these objects were accomplished.

The Lord Jesus had to bring to naught the power of sin. He could do this only in His own person. Therefore He came in the closest possible likeness of sinful flesh; in the weakness of flesh; with the fullest capacity to be tempted as we are. From His baptism with the Holy Spirit, and the temptation of Satan which followed, up to the fearful soul agony in Gethsemane, and the offering of Himself on the cross, His life was a ceaseless strife against self-will and self-honour; against the temptations of the flesh, and of the world, to reach His goal—the setting up of His kingdom—by fleshly or worldly means. Every day He had to take up and carry His Cross, that is, to lose His own life, and will, by going out of Himself and doing, and speaking nothing, save what he had seen or heard from the Father. That which took place in the temptation in the wilderness, and in the agony of Gethsemane—at the beginning and end of His public ministry—is only a peculiarly clear manifestation of the disposition which characterised His whole life. He was tempted to the sin of self-assertion but He overcame the temptation to satisfy lawful desires—from the first temptation, to obtain bread to satisfy His hunger, till the last, that He might not have to drink the bitter cup of death—that He might be subject to the will of the Father.

So He offered up Himself and His life; He denied Himself, and took up His Cross; He learned obedience and became perfect; in His own person He gained a complete victory over the power of sin, till He was able to testify that the evil one, " The prince of this world cometh and hath nothing in Me."

His death on the cross was the last and most glorious achievement in His personal victory over the power of sin, from this the atoning death of the cross derived its value. For a reconciliation was necessary, if guilt was to be removed. No one can contend with sin without at the same time coming into conflict with the wrath of God. These two cannot be separated from one another. The Lord Jesus desired to deliver man from his sin. He could not do this save by suffering death as Mediator, and in that death suffering the curse of God's wrath against sin, and bearing it away. But His supreme power to remove guilt and the curse did not lie merely in the fact that He endured so much pain and suffering of death, but that He endured it all *in willing obedience to the Father,* for the maintenance and glorification of His righteousness. It was this disposition of self-sacrifice, of bearing of the Cross willingly, which bestowed on the Cross its power.

So the Scripture says:—" He became obedient unto death, even the death of the cross. Wherefore God also hath highly exalted Him, and given Him a name above every name " (Phil. ii. 8, 9).

And again: " Yet learned He obedience by the things which He suffered; and being made perfect, He became the author of eternal salvation unto all them that obey Him " (Heb. v. 8, 9). It is because Jesus broke down and conquered the power of sin first in His personal life that He can remove from us the guilt of sin, and thus deliver us from both its power and guilt. The cross is the divine sign, proclaiming to us that the way, the only way to the life of God, is through the yielding up in sacrifice of the self-life.

Now this spirit of obedience, this sacrifice of self, which bestowed on the cross its infinite value, bestowed that value also on the blood of the cross. Here again God reveals to us the secret of the power of that blood. That blood is the proof of obedience unto death of the Beloved Son; of that disposition which chose to offer it (the blood), to shed it, to lose His own life rather than commit the sin of pleasing Himself; of the sacrifice of everything, even life itself, to glorify the Father. The life which dwelt in that blood—the heart from which it flowed—glowing with love and devotion to God and His will, was one of entire obedience and consecration to Him.

And, now, what do you think? If that blood, living and powerful through the Holy Spirit, comes into contact with our hearts, and if we rightly understand what the blood of the cross means, is it possible that that blood should not impart its holy nature to us? But as the blood could not have been shed apart from the sacrifice of " self " on the cross, so it cannot be received or enjoyed apart from a similar sacrifice of " self." That blood will bring to us a " self " sacrificing disposition, and in our work there will be a conformity to, and an imitation of, the crucified One, making self-sacrifice the highest and most blessed law of our lives. The blood is a living, spiritual, heavenly power. It will bring the soul that is entirely surrendered to it, to see and know by experience that there is no entrance into the full life of God, save by the self-sacrifice of the cross.

II. The Power Which the Cross has Obtained by this Disposition.

As we pay attention to this we shall have a deeper insight into the meaning of the Cross, and " the blood of the cross." The apostle Paul speaks of the word of the Cross as " the power of God."

We want to know what the Cross as the power of God can accomplish. We have seen the twofold relationship our Lord has towards sin. First, He must in Himself, as man, subdue its *power*; then He can destroy its effects before God, as *guilt*. The one was a process carried on through His whole life; the other took place in the hour of His passion. Now that He has completed His work, we may receive both blessings at the same time. Sin is a unity, so is redemption. We receive in an equal share, both deliverance from the power of sin, and acquittal from its guilt, at the same time. As far as consciousness is concerned, however, acquittal from guilt comes earlier than a clear sense of the forgiveness of sins. It cannot be otherwise. He (our Lord) had first to obtain the blotting out of guilt, through His victory over sin, and then He entered heaven. The blessing comes to us in the reverse order; redemption descends upon us as a gift from above, and therefore restoration of a right relationship to God comes first, deliverance from guilt; along with that, and flowing from it, comes deliverance from the power of sin.

This two-fold deliverance we owe to the power of the Cross. Paul speaks of the first, deliverance from guilt, in the words of our text. He says that God has become reconciled, " having made peace by the blood of the cross " with a view to reconciling all things to Himself.

Sin had brought about a change in God; not in His nature, but in His relationship towards us. He had to turn away from us in wrath. Peace has been made through the cross of Christ. By reconciliation for sin God has reconciled us with, and united us to Himself.

The power of the Cross in heaven has been manifested in the entire removal of everything that could bring about a separation from God, or awaken His wrath, so that in Christ we are granted the utmost freedom of entrance to, and the most intimate intercourse with God. Peace has been made, and proclaimed; peace reigns in heaven, we are perfectly reconciled to God, and have been received again into His friendship.

[39]

All this is through the power of the Cross. Oh, that we had eyes to see how completely the veil has been rent; how free and unhindered is our access to God; and how freely His blessing may flow towards us! There is now nothing, absolutely nothing, to hinder the fullness of the love and power of God from coming to us and working in us, save only our unbelief, our slowness of heart. Let us meditate upon the power which the blood has exercised in heaven, till our unbelief itself is conquered, and our right to these heavenly powers by faith, fills our lives with joy.

But the powerful effect of the Cross with God, in heaven, in the blotting out of guilt, and our renewed union with God, is, as we have seen—inseparable from that other effect— the breaking down of the authority of sin over man, by the sacrifice of " self." Therefore Scripture teaches us that the Cross not only works out a disposition or desire to make such a sacrifice, but it really bestows the power to do so, and completes the work. This appears with wonderful clearness in the Epistle to the Galatians. In one place the Cross is spoken of as the reconciliation for guilt. " Christ hath redeemed us from the curse of the law, being made a curse for us; for it is written, cursed is every one that hangeth on a tree " (Gal. iii. 13). But there are three other places where the Cross is even more plainly spoken of as the victory over the power of sin; as the power to put to death the " I " of the self life; of the flesh; and of the world. " I am crucified with Christ: nevertheless I live; yet not I, but Christ liveth in me " (Gal. ii. 20). " And they that are Christ's have crucified the flesh with the affections and lusts " (Gal. v. 24). " But God forbid that I should glory, save in the cross of our Lord Jesus Christ, by whom the world is crucified unto me, and I unto the world " (Gal. vi. 14). In these passages our union with Christ, the crucified One, and the conformity to Him resulting from that union, are represented as the result of the power exercised on us by the Cross.

To understand this we must remember that when Jesus chose the cross, and took it up, and carried it, and finally died on it, He did this as the second Adam, as the Head and Surety of His people. What He did, had and retains power for them, and exercises that power in those who understand and believe this. The life which He bestows on them is a life in which the cross is the most outstanding characteristic. Our Lord carried His cross all through His entire life as Mediator. By dying on that cross as Mediator, He obtained the life of glory. As the believer is united to Him and receives His life, he receives a life that, through the cross, has overthrown the power of sin, and he can henceforth say, "I am crucified with Christ." "I know that my old man is crucified with Christ"; "I am dead to sin"; "I have crucified the flesh"; "I am crucified to the world" (Rom. vi. 6, 11).

All these expressions from God's Word refer to something that occurred in a time now past. The Spirit and life of Jesus bestow on believers their share in the victory over sin which was achieved on the cross. And now in the power of this participation and fellowship they live as Jesus lived; they live always as those crucified to themselves; as those who know that their "old man," and "flesh" are crucified so as to be put to death. In the power of this fellowship they live as Jesus lived. They have the power in all things and all times to choose the Cross in spite of the "old man," and the world; to choose the Cross and to let it do its work.

The law of life for Jesus was the surrender of His own will to that of the Father, by giving up that life to death, so as to enter upon the heavenly life of redemption—by the cross, to the throne. So surely as there is a kingdom of sin, under the authority of which we were brought by our connection with the first Adam, so surely had there been set up a new kingdom of grace, in Christ Jesus, under the powerful influence of which we are brought by faith. The marvellous power by which Jesus subdued sin on the cross, lives and works in us, and not only calls us to life as He lived, but enables us to do so; to adopt the Cross as the motto and law of our lives.

Believer, that blood with which you have been sprinkled; under which you live daily, is the blood of the Cross. It obtains its power from the fact that it was the complete sacrifice of a life to God. The blood and the cross are inseparably united: The blood comes from the cross; it bears witness to the cross; it leads to the cross. The power of the Cross is in that blood; every touch of the blood should inspire you with a fresh ability to take the Cross as the law of your life. "Not my will but Thine be done" may, now, in that power, become a song of daily consecration. What the Cross teaches you, that it bestows upon you; what it imposes upon you, that it makes possible for you. Let the everlasting sprinkling of the blood of the cross be your choice, and through that blood, the disposition, as well as the power of the cross, will be seen in you.

III. The Love which the Cross Reveals, and which bestows upon us all that the Cross has gained.

We must now fix our attention on this, if we are to learn the full glory of the blood of the cross.

We have spoken of the disposition of which the cross is the expression, and of the powerful influence that disposition exercises in us and through us if we allow the blood of the cross to have its full power over us. The fear, however, often arises in the mind of a Christian that it is too much of a burden always to preserve and manifest that disposition; and even the assurance that the Cross is "the power of God" which produces this disposition does not entirely remove that fear, since the exercise of that power depends to some extent on our surrender and faith, and these are far from being what they ought to be. Can we find in the cross a deliverance from this infirmity, the healing of this disease? Cannot "the blood of the cross" make us partakers always, without ceasing, not only of the blotting out of guilt, but also of victory over the power of sin?

It can. Draw near, to hear once more what the Cross proclaims to you. It is only when we understand aright, and receive into our hearts the love of which the Cross speaks, that we can experience its full power and blessing. Paul indeed bears witness to this: "I am crucified with Christ; nevertheless I live; yet not I, but Christ liveth in me: and the life which I now live in the flesh I live by the faith of the Son of God, Who loved me, and gave Himself for me" (Gal. ii. 20).

Faith in the love of Him "who gave Himself for me" on the cross enables me to live as one who has been crucified with Him.

The cross is the revelation of love. He saw that there was no other way by which His love could redeem those whom He so loved, save by shedding His blood for them on the cross; it is because of this that He would not allow Himself to be turned aside by the terror of the cross, not even when it caused His soul to tremble and shudder. The cross tells us that He loved us so truly that His love surmounted every difficulty—the curse of sin, and the hostility of man— that His love has conquered, and has won us for Himself. The cross is the triumphant symbol of eternal love. By the cross love is seated on the throne, so that from the place of omnipotence it can now do for the beloved ones all that they desire.

What a new and glorious light is thus shed on the demand the Cross makes on me, and on what it offers to do for me; on the meaning, and glory, and life of the Cross, to which I have been called by the Word—I, whose flesh is so disposed to go astray that even the promise of the Spirit and the power of heaven seem insufficient to bestow on me the courage I need. But lo! here is something that is better still than the promise of power. The Cross points out to me the living

Jesus in His eternal, all-conquering love. Out of love to us He gave Himself up to the cross, to redeem a people for Himself. In this love He accepts of everyone who comes to Him in the fellowship of His cross, to bestow upon them all the blessings that He had obtained on that cross. And now He receives us in the power of His eternal and ever efficacious love, which ceases not for one moment to work out in us what He obtained for us on the cross.

I see it ! What we need is a right view of Jesus Himself, and of His all-conquering, eternal love. The blood is the earthly token of the heavenly glory of that love ; the blood points to that love. What we need is to behold Jesus Himself in the light of the cross. All the love manifested by the cross is the measure of the love He bears to us to-day. The love which was not terrified by any power or opposition of sin will now conquer everything in us that would be a hindrance. The love which triumphed on the accursed tree is strong enough to obtain and maintain a complete victory over us. The love manifested by " a Lamb as it had been slain in the midst of the throne," bearing always the marks of the cross, lives solely to bestow on us the disposition, and power, and the blessing of the cross. To know Jesus in His love, and to live in that love, to have the heart filled with that love, is the greatest blessing that the cross can bring to us. It is the way to the enjoyment of all the blessings of the cross.

Glorious Cross ! Glorious Cross, which brings to us, and makes known to us, the eternal love. The blood is the fruit and power of the cross ; the blood is the gift and be- stowal of that love. In what a full enjoyment of love those may now live who have been brought into such wonderful contact with the blood, who live every moment under its cleansing. How wondrously that blood unites us to Jesus and His love. He is the High Priest, out of whose heart that blood streamed, to whose heart that blood returns, who is Himself the end of the sprinkling of the blood, who Himself perfects the sprinkling of the blood in order that by it He may take possession of the heart that He on the cross had won. He is the High Priest who in the tenderness of love now lives to perfect everything in us, so that the disposition which the Cross has established as the law of our lives, and the victory which the Cross offers us as the power of our lives, may be realised by us.

Beloved Christian, whose hope is in the blood of the cross, give yourself up to experience its full blessing. Each drop of that blood points to the surrender and death of self-will, of the "I" life, as the way to God, and life in Him. Each drop of that blood assures you of the power of a life, a heavenly life, obtained by Jesus on the cross, to maintain that disposition, that crucified life, in you. Each drop of that blood brings Jesus, and His eternal love, to you, to work out all the blessing of the Cross in you, and to keep you in that love.

May each thought of the cross and the blood bring you nearer to your Saviour, and into a deeper union with Him to whom they point you.

CHAPTER IV

The Altar Sanctified by the Blood

" Seven days shalt thou make an atonement for the altar, and sanctify it ; and it shall be an altar most holy : whatsoever toucheth the altar shall be holy."—Exod. xxix. 37.

OF all the articles in the furnishing of the Tabernacle the altar was in many respects the most important. The golden mercy seat on which God manifested His visible glory in the Most Holy place within the veil, was more glorious—it was, however, hidden from the eyes of Israel, being the representation of the hidden presence of God in heaven. Only once in the year was Israel's active faith, intentionally, fixed on it. But at the altar, on the other hand, every day God's priests were continually engaged. The altar might be likened to a door of entrance to all the service of God, in the Holy Place.

Before there was either a temple or Tabernacle, an altar served as a place for the worship of God ; as in the case of Noah and the Patriarchs. Man may worship God without a temple, if he has an altar ; but he may not worship God without an altar—even if he has a temple. Before God spoke to Moses, at Sinai, about a Tabernacle where He might dwell among the people, He had already spoken to him about sacrificial worship. The service of the altar was the beginning, the centre, indeed the heart, of the service of the Tabernacle and temple.

Why was that ? What was the altar ? and why did it occupy such an important position ? The Hebrew word for " altar " gives the answer. It means, specially, the place of putting to death, of killing. Even the place of incense—where there was no slain victim—bore the name of altar, because gifts offered in sacrifice to God were laid upon it. The chief thought is this : that man's service for God consists in the sacrifice and consecration of himself and all he has to God. To this end there had to be a separated place, ordered and sanctified by God Himself. Because the altar was ordered and sanctified by Him, it sanctifies and makes the gift that is laid upon it acceptable. The offerer brings to it not only the sacrifice that is to atone for his sins, but also the thank-offering that follows reconciliation, as the expression of his love and thankfulness, and of his desire for closer fellowship with God; and for the full enjoyment of His favour. The altar is the place of sacrifice; of consecration; and also of fellowship with God.

The altar of the Old Testament must have an antitype in the New Testament; something that in spiritual worship is the perfect reality of which the Old Testament altar was only the shadow. "We have an altar" says the Holy Spirit, in Hebrews xiii. 10. In the eternal activities of heaven there is also an altar. "And another angel came and stood at the altar, having a golden censer . . . And the angel took the censer and filled it with fire of the altar" (Rev. viii. 3, 5). That altar in the New Testament no less than that of the Old Testament was a place for putting to death; a place of sacrifice. It is not difficult to tell where that place is which is spoken of in the New Testament. It is the altar, where, "once for all," the Lamb of God was sacrificed as the great sin-offering, where also each believer must present himself with all that he has as a thank-offering to God. That altar is the Cross.

In our text we learn that the altar itself had to be sanctified by blood, if it was to possess the power of sanctifying whatever touched it. Our text tells us of :—

I.   The Altar that was Sanctified by Blood.

II. The Offering that is Sanctified by the Altar.

May the Spirit of God open our eyes to see the full power of the blood of the Cross, in the sanctification of the Cross as the place of our death, where we also may be consecrated to God.

I. The Altar Sanctified by Blood.

It is in the midst of the instructions concerning the consecration of Aaron as High Priest (his sons being consecrated with him as priests) that the words of the text appear. A priest must have an altar. But just as the priest himself had to be sanctified by blood, so was it also with the altar. God commanded that a sin-offering should be prepared to cleanse the altar and to make atonement for it.

For seven days Moses had to carry on this work of making atonement for the altar.

We read : "And Moses took the blood (of the sin-offering), and put it upon the horns of the altar round about, with his finger, and purified the altar, and poured the blood at the bottom of the altar, and sanctified it, to make reconciliation upon it " (Lev. viii. 15). By this " reconciliation," not only was the altar sanctified, and made " holy," but it was made " most holy "—" A holy of holies." This expression is the same as that used to describe the inner shrine of the Tabernacle where God dwelt. It is used here of the altar ; which had a similar, special measure of holiness. The one was the hidden, the other the approachable " Holy of Holies." Then we read: "Whatsoever toucheth the altar shall be holy " (Exod. xxx. 37). By the sevenfold atoning with blood the altar had obtained such a holiness that it had the power of sanctifying everything that was laid upon it. The Israelite had no need to fear that his offering might be too small or too unworthy ; the altar sanctified the gift that was laid upon it. Our Lord referred to this, as a well-known fact, when He asked, " Whether is greater, the gift, or the altar that sanctifieth the gift ? " (Matt. xxiii. 19). The altar, by the sevenfold sprinkling of the blood, sanctified every offering which was laid upon it.

What a glorious fresh light this word sheds on " the power of the blood of Jesus," and on His cross, that is sanctified by it. We have already inquired how it is that the blood obtained its value from the cross. As blood—proof of the surrender of the life of Christ in obedience unto death—it has power to make reconciliation, and to obtain victory over sin. But lo !—here, a fresh glory of the blood is revealed to us. The cross on which it was shed is not only the altar on which Jesus was sacrificed, but it has been consecrated by that blood as an altar on which we also may be sacrificed and made acceptable to God.

It is the Cross alone, as sanctified by blood—(yes, sanctified to be a " holy of holies," which sanctifies everything that touches it)—that has this power.

In heathen worship, and also in Romanism, people are often taught a doctrine about a cross ; that by self-imposed suffering, and self-sacrifice, they may become pleasing to God. But they seek a value in the sufferings themselves, as a putting to death of the flesh. They do not understand that everything that man does, whether it be suffering, or sacrifice, is stained by sin, and is thus incapable of really conquering sin, or pleasing God. They do not understand that even the cross itself, as the means of self-sacrifice, must first be sanctified. Before the sufferings of a cross can sanctify us, it must itself first be sanctified.

For this purpose God made a most glorious provision. He caused an altar to be erected for which a sevenfold and thus a perfect reconciliation had been made, so that whatever touched that altar was holy. By the blood of the Son of God the cross has become " most holy " : " A holy of holies," with power to sanctify us.

We know how this has been accomplished. We cannot too often speak or think about it, nor believe it or be thankful enough for it—by shedding His precious, divine blood as a sacrifice for our sin, by surrendering Himself in perfect obedience to the will of the Father, and by a personal victory over sin, by bearing our punishment and curse, Jesus has conquered sin, and rendered it powerless for us also.

What Jesus did and suffered on the cross, He did and suffered as the Second Adam, as our Surety, our Head. He showed us there that the only way to be freed from the flesh— in the likeness and weakness of which He came—so as to enter into the life of God and of the Spirit, was by surrendering the flesh to the righteous judgment of God. The only way into the life of God was through the death of the flesh.

But not merely did He show us that this was the only way, but by His death He obtained the right and power to enable us to walk in that very way. Our natural life is so entirely under the authority of sin that we cannot be delivered from it by any sufferings or sacrifices or endeavours of our own. But the life and sufferings of Jesus have such a divine power, that by them the authority of sin has been entirely destroyed, and everyone who seeks the way to God, and to the life of God, through sacrifice and death in fellowship with Him, will find that way, and be enabled to walk in it.

Through the blood of Jesus ; through the perfect reconciliation and the power of an eternal life which His blood has revealed ; the Cross of Jesus has been sanctified for ever as an altar on which alone everything that is presented to God must be offered.

The Cross is an altar. We have seen that the altar is the the place for slaying, the place of sacrifice. The place where the incense was offered was also called an altar. On both the altar of sacrifice and the altar of incense a fire burned. What is presented to God must first pass through death and then be consumed by fire. In its natural condition it is unclean ; by death judgment upon sin must be executed ; it must be consumed by fire, and in a new, spiritual form borne heavenwards.

What the altar of sacrifice—what the Cross proclaims about Christ, is the law in the temple of a Holy God—there is no way to God save through death, through the sacrifice of life. There is no way to God nor to heaven for us save by the Cross.

And the Cross is not merely that cross on which we are to believe that Jesus died for our sins. No, but as the Cross on which we must die. The Lord Jesus early and repeatedly warned His disciples that He must be crucified, and that they must bear their Cross after Him ; each must be prepared to be crucified even as He was. He did not mean by that merely outward suffering or death ; no, He spoke of the inner self-denial, of the hating and losing the self-life as the fellowship of His Cross. This was before His crucifixion. The Holy Spirit teaches us by the apostle Paul how we are to speak about the Cross after Jesus had been put to death on it :—" I am crucified with Christ " ; " They that are Christ's have crucified the flesh with its affections and lusts " ; " God forbid that I should glory, save in the Cross of our Lord Jesus Christ, by whom the world is crucified unto me, and I unto the world." These three passages in the epistle to the Galatians teach us that we are not to regard the sufferings on the cross as being only the expiation of our guilt, but as the characteristic and the power of our lives. In the cross, the life of Jesus on earth attained its purpose, its climax, its perfection ; apart from the cross He could not have been the Christ. The life of Christ from heaven bears the same characteristic in us ; it is the life of the crucified One. The phrase " I am crucified with Christ " is inseparable from the other which follows : " Christ liveth in me " ; each day and each hour we must abide in the place of crucifixion ; each moment the power of the Cross of Christ must work in us ; we must be made conformable unto His death. Then the power of God will be manifested in us ; the weakness and death of the Cross is ever coupled with the life and power of God. Paul says :—" For though He (Christ) was crucified through weakness, yet He liveth by the power of God. For we also are weak in Him, but we shall live with Him by the power of God toward you " (2 Cor. xiii. 4).

Many Christians do not understand this. The cross in which they glory differs from that in which Paul gloried. He gloried in a Cross on which not only Christ was crucified, but on which he himself was also crucified. They glory in a cross on which Christ died, but they are not willing to die on it themselves. Yet this is what God designs. The very blood that atoned for us on the cross has sanctified the cross that we, in fellowship with our Lord on it, might find the way of life.

Notice how clearly this distinction and this connection between the blood of atonement and the sacrifice of the flesh is taught us in the well-known passage, " Having therefore, brethren, boldness to enter into the holiest by the blood of Jesus, by a new and living way, which He hath consecrated for us, through the veil, that is to say, His flesh. Let us draw near . . . " (Heb. x. 19-22). " The new and living way " is a different thing from " boldness through the blood." It is the way in which Jesus Himself walked, rending the veil of His flesh when He shed His blood, and which He by so doing has consecrated for us. This way always passes through the rent veil of the flesh. The crucifixion and sacrifice of the flesh was the way in which the blood was shed. Everyone who obtains a share in that blood is, by that blood, brought into this way. It is the way of the Cross. Nothing less than the entire sacrifice of one's self-life is the way to the life of God. The Cross with its entire renunciation of self is the only altar on which we can consecrate ourselves to God.

The Cross has been sanctified by the blood of Jesus as the altar on which we may become a sacrifice, holy and acceptable to God.

And now we see the meaning of that phrase which is connected with the altar, and also with the Cross, " Whatsoever toucheth the altar shall be holy" (Exod. xxix. 37). The smallness or unworthiness of the offering of him who brought it did not render it unacceptable to God. The altar, sanctified by blood, had the power to make it holy. And thus when I fear lest my self-sacrifice be not indeed perfect, or lest in my dying to "self" I may not be entirely honest and true, my thoughts must be turned away from myself, and fixed on the wonderful power which the blood of Jesus has bestowed on His Cross, to sanctify all that touches it. The Cross—the crucified Jesus—is the power of God : when I, by increasing insight into what the Cross means, really choose it, and hold it fast, then there proceeds from the Cross, by the Spirit of Jesus, a power of life to take me up and hold me fast that I may live as one who has been crucified.

Each moment I may walk in the consciousness of my crucifixion, my entire renunciation of self because the Spirit of the crucified One makes His Cross the death of the self-life and the power of the new life of God that rises out of death. From the Cross as a sanctified altar a sanctifying power is exercised over me. From the moment that I trustfully surrender myself to the Cross I become a sanctified person— one of God's saints. And in proportion as I believe in the sanctifying power of the Cross, and seek to live in fellowship with it, I become partaker of a progressive and increasing holiness. The Cross on which I have been crucified with Jesus becomes daily the altar which sanctifies everything that touches it, and sanctifies me also, with a divine sanctification. The altar sanctified by blood, sanctifies the gift laid upon it.

But we must now closely consider :—

II. The Offerings Which are Sanctified by the Altar.

The altar is sanctified by blood, that in time it may sanctify the gift that is laid upon it. What is the gift which we have to lay on the altar ? We find the answer in a word of Paul written to the Romans—" I beseech you therefore brethren, by the mercies of God, that ye present your bodies a living sacrifice, holy, acceptable unto God " (Rom. xii. 1). The body of the victim was laid upon the altar. Christ bore our sins in His body on the tree. Our bodies are the sacrifices which we have to present to God, on the altar. The body has many members, and is a wonderful union of several powers. Each of these separately, and all together, must be laid on the altar.

The body has a head—we speak of the head with the brains as the seat of understanding. The head with all its thoughts must be laid on the altar. I must consecrate my understanding entirely to the service of God; placing it entirely under His control and direction, to be used by Him: I must " bring into captivity every thought to the obedience of Christ " (2 Cor. x. 5).

The head has its members also, the eyes, and mouth, and ears. By the eye I come into touch with the visible world, and its desires; the eyes must be turned away from vanity, and be wholly His, to see, or not to see, according to His will. By the ear, I enter into fellowship with my fellow men. The ear must be consecrated to the Lord, and is not to listen to language or conversation that pleases my flesh— but it is to be attentive to the voices which the Lord sends to me. By my mouth I reveal what is in me, what I think, and seek, and will; by it I exercise an influence over others: mouth and tongue and lips must be consecrated so as not to speak except according to the will of God, and to His glory. The eye, the ear, the mouth, the head, and all belonging to it, must be laid on the altar to be purified and sanctified by the Cross.

I must renounce every right to manage them; I must acknowledge my utter sinfulness, and want of strength to control or sanctify them; I must believe that He who purchased them will accept of them and guard them in the fellowship of His Cross and of His entire surrender of Himself. In that faith I must offer them to God upon the altar. The blood has sanctified the altar and made it " the Holy of Holies " : all that touches the altar becomes holy. The act of touching is a living, spiritual, real, and for faith, an ever-enduring thing. The reconciliation of the Cross has opened the way for the fellowship of the Cross. The blood has sanctified the Cross as my altar.

The body has also hands and feet. The hands represent power to work. My handiwork, my business, my service, my possessions must all be placed upon the altar to be sanctified, cleansed from sin, and consecrated to God. My feet represent my ways and my walk; the paths I choose, the companionship which I cultivate, and the places which I visit. The feet, sanctified by the altar, cannot any longer go their own way, they have been presented to God to be in all things under His leading, and at His service, and they must " be beautiful " to carry the good news, and to bring help to the sorrowful and the lost. With hands and feet bound, the body must be laid upon the altar, not having the least freedom to stir, till He enables the soul to cry out, "I am Thy servant; Thou hast loosened my bands " (Ps. cxvi. 16).

Our Saviour hung on the cross, nailed to it by hands and feet; in wonderful spiritual union with Him, hands and feet are crucified with Him; the natural, sinful use of them is condemned, and abides daily under that sentence; in the sanctifying power of the Cross of the living Christ, they are free and holy, and fit to work for God.

The body has a heart, the centre of life, where the blood, in which the soul dwells, flows in and out. In the heart is the meeting place of all the desires and endeavours of men; of all they will or choose; of love and hatred. The heart of Jesus was pierced on the cross. Everything that flows in or out of our heart must be laid upon the altar. I must renounce the right to seek or will anything after my own wish; to love or hate after my own desire. In the case of Jesus the cross meant: " My will is of no account: the will of God is everything "; "the will of God, cost what it may, must be done, even if it costs my life." In the smallest as well as in the greatest things God's will must be done. In nothing must my will be done—in everything God's will.

[55]

That is the writing above the cross which Jesus sanctified as an altar for us. The will is the kingly power of the heart. It is governed by our love or hatred, and by it in turn, the whole man is governed. When the will is on the altar, that is, on the Cross, the fellowship of the Cross will soon extend its power over the whole man. My will, sinful and blind; my will, condemned and freely surrendered to death; my will, put to death on the Cross; my will in fellowship with Jesus living again, and raised to life again, and made free; my will now entirely submitted to His leading and authority, this is the way in which the believing heart comes to understand what it means to be on the Cross as on an altar. And the believer experiences that the two seemingly opposed conditions are united, in a glorious union : his will bound to the Cross, and yet free; his will, dead on the Cross, and yet alive. And so the truth now first becomes glorious even for him, " I am crucified with Christ "—" Christ liveth in me " and " I live by faith."

Heart and head, hands and feet together form one body. They are united in that wonderful structure of flesh in which the soul has her lodging. It was created at first to be the servant of the soul, to be kept in subjection to the guidance of the spirit; sin subverted this order. The sensual body became the seducer or tempter of the soul, and has dragged the spirit down into servitude. The only way for the restoration of the order which God ordained is for the body to be placed upon the altar; the body by the Holy Spirit to be nailed to the Cross. The body with its eating and drinking; with its sleeping and working; with its wonderful system of nerves by which the soul comes into contact with the world—the body must go to the altar. The power of the Cross of Christ which by the Holy Spirit becomes at once and continuously active, must have authority over the entire body; the body, with the soul and spirit dwelling in it, must become a living sacrifice to God. Thus that word of deep significance obtains its fulfilment : " the body for the Lord: and the Lord for the body" (1 Cor. vi. 13).

Beloved Christian, when we gather at the Lord's Table— to meet with Him, to receive Him who was sacrificed on the cross for us—what our Lord asks us to do is to offer ourselves to Him and for Him. What will He do for us? He will receive us into the fellowship of His Cross, as the most glorious thing He possesses, by which He entered into the glory of the Father. In the statement concerning the altar sanctified by blood so that it may in turn sanctify the gift, He points out the way and the place, where we may find Him.

Are you willing to ascend the altar, the place of death? Are you willing to make the Cross your abode, the place where you will pass every hour of your life in fellowship with the crucified Jesus? Or does it seem to you to be too hard to surrender yourself, your will, your life so utterly up to death, so as to bear about daily the dying of the Lord Jesus? I pray you do not think this is too hard for you. It is the only way to close fellowship with the blessed Jesus; and through Him a free entrance to the Eternal Father and His love.

It need not be too difficult for you! In fellowship with Jesus it will become joy and salvation. I pray you, become willing; let us ascend to the altar to die so that we may live. Or is it your fear that you are not fit to complete such a sacrifice? Listen then to the glorious comfort which the word of God gives you to-day "the altar sanctifies the gift." By the sevenfold reconciliation, even the Old Testament altar had power to sanctify every gift which was laid upon it. "How much more shall the blood of Christ, who through the eternal Spirit offered Himself without spot to God" sanctify the Cross as an altar on which the sacrifice of your body may be sanctified? You have learned about the wonderful power of the precious blood, how it has conquered sin and has opened the way into "the Holiest,"

[57]

and being sprinkled in that Most Holy place, before God, it has made His throne a throne of grace.

It is the very same word which is used concerning that inner "Most Holy place," and the altar. Both are called "the Holy of Holies." What the blood has accomplished by its wonderful power in the unseen Holy of Holies in destroying the authority of sin in God's sight, that also is accomplished in the "Holy of Holies" on which you are to be offered up. In the Holy of Holies where God dwells, the blood by its wonderful power has perfected everything : in your "Holy of Holies" where you must dwell—the altar— it works with no less power. Lay yourself down upon that altar. Trust the sanctifying power of the blood communicated to the altar. Believe that the blood and the Cross are inseparable from the living Jesus, as High Priest, and from His Spirit as fire, and you will receive the assurance that the sanctifying of the gift by the altar is so divine and powerful that you will reckon upon a victory over all your uncleanness and weakness. Lay yourself down upon the altar as the altar of consecration and approval. The altar is the place of the blessed presence of God ; dying with Christ leads to a life with Him in the love of the Father.

It has sometimes been said that as Jesus is Priest and Offering, He must also be the altar. There is a truth in this representation. The Cross exists not apart from the crucified Christ. At the Cross the living Christ is found. If this representation helps your faith, take the crucified Christ as your altar, and lay down your body with all that it contains, with all the life that dwells in it, on Him, before the Father. Then you are a living, holy sacrifice, acceptable to God. Then you will reach the full fellowship of which the Lord's Supper is the type.

"The bread which we break, is it not the fellowship of the body of Christ ? The cup which we drink, is it not the fellowship of the blood of Christ ? " Full fellowship with the crucified flesh and the shed blood is what He desires

ip is found when we give our-
as He died, so that we may live
e, when we lay ourselves on the
to the Cross to become one by
us.

ltar; the altar sanctifies the gift.
the altar is sanctified. I beseech
od that ye present your bodies a
table to God.

CHAPTER V.

Faith in the Blood

" Whom God hath set forth to be a Propitiation through faith in His blood "—Rom. iii. 25.

IN the course of our inquiry as to what the Scriptures teach concerning the power of the blood of Jesus, it has become clear to us, from many indications, that the truth referring to the blood is the central point of the revelation of God as touching human redemption.

Faith in the blood of Christ is the one thing which makes the doctrines of the holiness and grace of God, of the divine and human nature of Christ, of our deliverance from sin and union with God, intelligible. In the history of the kingdom of God covering the period from the first to the second Paradise, as well as in the experience of each believer, it becomes manifest that we have in the blood of Christ the supreme revelation of the wisdom, the power, and the love of God.

Let us gather up what we have already learned, and endeavour to set forth briefly and clearly its practical importance, taking by way of introduction the words of our text, " through faith in His blood." The Apostle uses these words with special reference to one particular effect of the blood—Reconciliation, which as we have seen underlies all its other effects, and so these words may be confidently applied to everything that Scripture elsewhere teaches concerning the blood. If we obtain a better understanding and make a fuller inward appropriation of these words, our labour will not be in vain. May the Lord our God grant us the teaching of His Holy Spirit while we consider :—

    I.   The Faith by which we become Partakers of the Power of the Blood.

    II. The Blood by which Faith manifests its Power to enjoy the Blood-bought Blessing.

I. The Faith by which we become Partakers of the Power of the Blood.

"Be it unto thee according to thy faith." We know that this foundation law of the kingdom of grace is applicable to every circumstance of the spiritual life. Faith is a disposition of heart, without which God's most glorious blessing is offered to us in vain; but by which, on the other hand, all the fullness of God's grace can be most certainly received and enjoyed. It is therefore of great importance for us to remind ourselves of those things which are necessary for a right exercise of that faith in the precious blood, by which alone we can press through to the enjoyment of all that the blood has obtained for us; but before considering these things it must be noted that faith is born from a sense of need.

The great event which moved heaven, earth, and hell; for which the world had to be prepared and for which it had to wait for four thousand years; the results of which will endure for ever—the shedding of the blood of the Son of God on the cross—had an unspeakably great object:— It was to bring about the destruction of sin itself, and of its consequences.

Only he who is in agreement with this object, and who seeks to attain it, is capable of entering into the full fellowship of faith in the blessing of that blood. He who desires to be delivered only from the punishment of sin, or from sin as far as it unfits him for heaven, is certainly not in a condition to appropriate by a strong faith, what the Word promises through the blood. But when the soul truly seeks, above everything else, to be cleansed *from sin itself*, and to live in abiding fellowship with a holy God—truly surrendering itself, with a fixed intention of experiencing all that is possible to be experienced in appropriating the power of the blood— it possesses the first requisite for a true faith in it. The deeper the dissatisfaction with what is wrong and deficient in our spiritual lives, the stronger the longing to be really delivered from sin; the more lively the desire to have unbroken intercourse in the presence of God in "the Holiest," so much the more is such a soul prepared to receive by faith what God promises, and will bestow. Oh! if our eyes were only opened to see what God is willing to become to us; if wandering and alienation from God became entirely unbearable; if the whole soul thirsted and cried out for the living God and His love; then salvation "through faith in His blood" would acquire a new meaning, and a new desire for it would be awakened.

Where the sense of need exists, the first requisite for a full faith in the blood is :—

i. A spiritual knowledge of the Word of God.

As surely as mere knowledge of the Word, by itself, profits but little, so surely faith cannot grow and become strong, apart from the Word applied by the Holy Spirit. There are many who think that as they have always hoped in the blood, as the ground of their salvation, there could not be much more for them still to learn about it. They are convinced that they are well acquainted with, and hold fast, the teaching of the Church, and they do not expect the Word to unlock anything new for them about the blood. They think so because they have so little understanding of what it means to place themselves under the guidance of the Holy Spirit, so that He, by His heavenly teaching, might inspire the well-known words or truths of Scripture with a new meaning.

They forget that it is only "the anointing" that teaches all things (1 John ii. 27), and that "we have received the Spirit which is of God that we might know the things that are freely given to us of God" (1 Cor. ii. 12).

The believer who desires to understand aright the efficacious and blessed power of the blood must submit entirely to the teaching of the Word through the Holy Spirit, in private. He must understand that the words of God have a much wider meaning than man himself can attach to them; and that the matters on which God speaks have a reality and power and glory of which he himself can form no conception; but the Holy Spirit will teach him to understand these things —not at once, but only as he devotes time and takes trouble to learn.

Believing in the rich, spiritual, living content of each Word of God, the learner must understand that " the blood of the Son of God " is a subject the glory of which God alone knows, and He alone can reveal. He must believe it is possible for each effect which is ascribed to the blood, to be brought about by a manifestation of divine power that is beyond our conception. In this attitude of mind he should take up, and meditate on, first what one portion of Scripture says about the blood, and then what another portion says, so that the Holy Spirit may apply to his soul something of its life-giving power. It is only by such a use of " the Word," in dependence upon the teaching of the Holy Spirit, that faith can be strengthened so as to recognise and receive what the blood has to bestow.

By this means it will be experienced how necessary it is to devote time to these things. Time must be found for meditation on the Word in private, so that it may sink into the heart. To read a portion, to get hold of a fresh thought, and then to go away in the hope that a blessing will follow, is of little use. The soul must give the Word time, in silence before God, to get fixed in the heart, otherwise it will be driven away again by the rush of the world. The thought may remain but there will be no power. Time must be given not merely occasionally, but regularly and persistently. Day after day, perhaps week after week, I must place myself under and give myself up to " the Word " which I desire to appropriate. It can become in reality the possession of my soul only by obtaining a lodging place in, and by becoming part of, my spiritual being. It is thus " faith cometh by the Word of God."

[63]

ii. In contradistinction to the Word is the real activity of the faith of appropriation, or, rather, of surrender to be appropriated. Faith is the *ear* which hears and receives the Word of God. It listens attentively to understand what God says. Faith is the *eye* which seeks to place before itself, as an object of vital importance, and, in its true perspective, what would otherwise remain only a thought. Faith thus sees the invisible : it observes the things which are not seen : it is the sure evidence of these things. Faith is accustomed to surround itself with, and to dwell in the midst of, those things which the Word leads the understanding to regard as heavenly realities. So it seeks to behold, in spirit, the blood being brought into heaven and sprinkled upon the throne and, by the Spirit, sprinkled upon the soul, with powerful results.

But faith is not only an ear and eye to ascertain but it is also *hand* and *mouth* to receive. What it hears from the Word, what it in spirit beholds, it appropriates to itself. Faith surrenders itself to the impression produced by what is heard, places itself under the influence of invisible objects, until they have secured for themselves a lodging in the heart, in their heavenly, life-giving power. Faith accepts it as a certainty that what the Word of God says, the power of God is prepared to make objectively real.

Faith knows that when it accepts the Word but has not yet had the longed-for experience, this is only because it is not yet strong enough to become inwardly partaker of what it had appropriated. It does not permit this in any way to dishearten it, but only devotes itself the more to persevere, till the undivided soul opens itself to receive the blessing. It knows that trust must always be coupled with surrender, and if there is postponement, it is only till the surrender is complete, and then faith will surely be crowned.

It is not difficult for us to obtain the appropriation of all the blessings of full salvation " through faith in His blood." Of each different word which is used in Scripture concerning the blood—" redemption," " cleansing," " sanctifi-cation," " redeemed," " cleansed," " sanctified," " pur-chased," " brought nigh by the blood "—faith says : " This word contains a heavenly, divine meaning, richer and deeper than I am able to grasp ; but the subject itself which is spoken of, as God understands it, the blessing in its heavenly power, is mine. God Himself will, by His divine power, make this matter real to me. I dare confidently to reckon on that—this blessing, in a sense that surpasses all human understanding, is mine. I must simply await God's time. I have only to live after the Spirit, and by Him be led, surrendering myself wholly, so that God may take possession of me. He Himself will bring this blessing to me in its full power."

iii. It is in fellowship with the Lord Jesus Himself that faith can be exercised and strengthened. It is a matter too little understood, that God bestows salvation upon us, in no other way, than *in*—not just *through*, but in—the Saviour. The living Jesus is salvation. He Who gave and now imparts His blood, He Himself it is, in Whom we must daily find our life and our salvation. Further, it is only in living direct fellowship with Him that our faith can increase and triumph. Many Christians take great pains in endeavouring to reach a life of full faith by earnest association with the Word, or by straining all their powers to believe, and yet they see but little fruit as the result of their efforts. The reason often is that, in studying the Word, and in trying to believe, they have not first of all found rest themselves in the love of the Saviour. Faith in God is an act of the spiritual life. It is Christ Who is our life, and Who imparts faith to us. He does this, however, not as an act or gift separate from Himself ; but in fellowship with Him faith is active. He is " the author and finisher of faith " : those who walk with Him learn from Him to exercise faith, they know not how. In the face of Jesus, the light which leads to " the full assurance of faith " is always found : to gaze upon His face, to sit

E [65]

still at His feet that the light of His love may shine upon the soul, is a sure way of obtaining a strong faith. He who longs for such a faith in order to come to the knowledge of the full power of the blood, needs only to practise this fellowship.

The shedding of His blood was the proof of His unspeakable love towards us. " He gave Himself for us that He might redeem us from all iniquity, and purify unto Himself a people for His own possession " (Titus ii. 14). His blood is the power by which He takes possession of us for Himself, to sanctify us. All that is necessary for the more powerful operation of the blood in us, is that faith in it should become wider, brighter, and stronger. He who longs for such a full faith will find it only, but find it certainly, in fellowship with Jesus. It is His work to impart the blood ; it is His work also to increase faith. Let there only be an undivided surrender to the Lord Jesus, the sacrifice of the " self " life—" I "—in order to walk with Him ; in that walk unbelief will wither.

This undivided surrender, however, is indispensable. True faith always includes entire surrender. To believe with the whole heart means to surrender with the whole heart to that Jesus in Whom life and salvation are. The will and the law of the Lord Jesus are inseparable from His person, and from His love : we cannot know nor receive Him without knowing and receiving His will : obedience is the one sure characteristic of the surrender of faith. Faith that is not coupled with obedience is an imagination, or pretence ; there is not a true surrender to Christ.

But the faith in which this true surrender is found, presses ever on to a deeper insight into what the blood means, and to the experience of what it can do. The blood is the life power of such a faith, for by it, it was quickened to an ever more glorious experience of its blessed sufficiency.

II. The Blood by which Faith manifests its Power to enjoy the Blood-bought Blessing. This is the second point demanding our attention.

We will not repeat what has already been said about the different effects of the blood, but point out some special characteristics of the way in which the blood accomplishes its work. Faith, however, must first be aroused to recognise and appropriate the fact that the blessed effects of the blood make all things possible, are ever enduring, and all inclusive.

i. All things are possible: The blood has a divine efficacy.

We have several times spoken of the wonderful power which the blood of Jesus manifested immediately after He had shed it. It was by that blood that Jesus, in His holy, triumphal march, broke open the doors of death and Hades, and carried its prisoners out with Him; that, then, as conqueror, He might see the doors of heaven thrown open for " the blood "—and that He might take possession of the Holy of Holies of God, on our behalf. With a similar wonderful power to that which the blood then manifested in making Reconciliation for sin, in removing its curse, in opening the Holiest, in restoring fellowship with God, it works to-day. With the very same power which was then manifested in those supreme things—concerning sin and its authority, concerning God and His law, concerning hell and heaven—with the very same power, the divine blood works now when sprinkled on a single soul.

That its divine efficacy is too little experienced we must confess. But this is because of our unbelief. If it were not for this unbelief, the mere thought of being ransomed and cleansed by the blood of God's own Son would cause our souls to leap for joy, and to overflow with love. Would not every exercise of faith in the blood cause the sense of the favour and nearness of God, the glory of deliverance from the curse and dominion of sin, to flow through the soul?

[67]

But, alas ! we may hear and think and sing about the blood, while it exercises almost no influence over us. Even the very thought that the blood always manifests such wonderful divine power seems strange and unreal to many, and so no wonderful work is done in us because of unbelief.

Our faith must be quickened to expect the all-conquering power of the blood. Even if there does not at once come a change in our feelings, nor any sensation of new blessing, let us commence in perfect quietness to fix our hearts on these truths of God. When the blood is made efficacious through the Spirit, it operates with a divine power either for reconciliation, or union with God, or sanctification. Let us believe, and still believe, and ever keep on believing, in the infinite power of the blood. Such faith will not be in vain. Although it may not be in the way, nor at the time we expected, we shall be brought into a new and deeper experience of salvation " through faith in the blood." Let us but seek with our whole heart to hold fast the truth : what the blood does, it does with a divine power.

ii. Next to its power to make all things possible, our faith must be assured of the ever enduring efficacy of the blood.

We have already seen on what foundation faith is grounded. By the Eternal Spirit the blood was once for all offered, by the Eternal High Priest it is administered in the power of an endless life : the power of the blood is eternally active. There is no single moment in which the blood is not exerting its full power. In the heavenly Holy of Holies where the blood is, before the throne, everything exists in the power of eternity, without cessation, or diminution. All activities in the heavenly Temple are on our behalf, and the effects are conveyed to us by the Holy Spirit. He is Himself the Eternal Spirit, and has been bestowed on us to make us partakers of all that has been, or will be done, in the Holiest by our Lord Jesus for us. He is able to make us partakers, in a very efficacious and blessed way, of the unceasing and continuous activities of the blood which never for one moment cease. If we long to abide always in the full enjoyment of close fellowship with God, Whom we serve as priests; if we desire to experience the constant cleansing of our souls from the stains of sin by the blood; if we wish to know the peace, or joy, or power, of the Cross of Jesus in the fellowship of His blood; all these things are possible because the eternal, never ceasing activities which the blood exercises in heaven may be exercised also in our hearts, here on earth.

The blessedness of a clear insight into these truths is very great. The general complaint, made by believers about their spiritual lives, is that they are conscious of their instability. They have a strong desire that the glorious experiences of special hours should be the continuous state of their mind, and it is God's will that it should be so. If you who desire this will only set your heart on something surpassing all that you have hitherto experienced, and fix your attention on the Holy of Holies now opened, with its heavenly life, and eternal redemption; and on the unchangeable priesthood of your Lord Jesus; then you will see that the divine provision for your unbroken enjoyment of His fellowship is perfect.

In the morning before you go out to your work, and to meet the distractions of the day, commit yourself to Him Who ever remains the same, that He may reveal in you the ever living activity of His blood, and He will do it. During the hours of business, when you can think of nothing else, the blessed results of the sprinkling of the blood and the nearness of God, of cleansing, of victory over sin, will be made yours. Our activity of faith must be an abiding thing, but not in the sense that we must anxiously take care to think about it every moment. No, not that; but in such a way that we, from the depths of our souls, cherish a quiet and steadfast confidence that " eternal redemption " has taken possession of us, and holds us fast by its heavenly activity, if only we are trustful. Thank God, we need not fear; each moment, without ceasing, we may live here below in the enjoyment of the blessing which the blood has procured for us because the effects of the blood are ever-enduring.

iii. Not less are we to believe in the all-embracing, all-penetrating power of the blood.

When the Priests were separated to their ministry, the blood was placed upon the tip of the ear, on the thumb of the hand, and on the toe of the foot. Possession was taken of the entire man for God; all his powers were sanctified: his ear to listen to, and for, God; his hand to work by, and for, God; his foot to walk with God, and to go out in His service. In the case of the believer, the precious blood of Christ will exercise a similar authority over every power, to sanctify it for the service of the Lord.

Christians have often had to complain about a divided life: there are certain portions of life or of work which are a hindrance in a walk with God. The only way to obtain deliverance from this is to see that the blood covers everything. "Almost all things are by the law purged with blood" (Heb. ix. 22). The entire person of the believer, with all his circumstances and affairs, must be brought into the Holy of Holies.

It is evident that, to enjoy such an experience, a most complete surrender to the Lord is necessary. The Priest who was marked by blood on the ear, hand, and foot, so that all the activities of these members might be sanctified, had to recognise that he had been separated to the service of God. The believer must give himself up no less wholly to be and live only for Jesus. In each relationship of his life, his home, his business, commercial or political affairs, he must give himself up to be led by the Holy Spirit, to live according to the law of God, and for His glory. Then the blood in its reconciling, cleansing, and sanctifying power will embrace everything; the peace of God, and the consciousness of His nearness, will, by the power of the heavenly life, reveal itself in all things. He will experience the completeness

[70]

of his deliverance from the authority of sin, of his liberty to enter upon a walk in the light and love of a Holy God. But always on this one condition: everything must be brought into the Holy of Holies, and set right there. The whole life must be spent there, for that is where the blood is and where it exercises its power. This, again, is by faith; faith that is absorbed in the contemplation of what the blood has accomplished in the Holy of Holies, and what power it now exercises there; and that, because of this, maintains on the authority of the Word, that all this power can be brought into uninterrupted contact with the personal life.

And then in proportion as the believer learns, in his own experience, how far-reaching the effects of the all-including blood are, his heart will be opened to long for a widespread experience of the power of the blood in the world around him.

"It pleased the Father that in Him should all fullness dwell; and having made peace through the blood of the cross, by Him to reconcile all things to Himself, whether they be things on earth or things in heaven" (Col. i. 19). The power of the blood avails for every creature, for those also who have "counted the blood of the Covenant wherewith they were sanctified an unholy thing" (Heb. x. 29), and for those who are "denying the Lord that bought them" (2 Pet. ii. 1). The experience of what the blood can accomplish for those who believe, will teach them to regard their fellow-men as living under the tender mercy of God, under redemption, and under the call to salvation through the precious blood. It will fill them with an irresistible impulse to devote their lives, which have been bought by blood and consecrated to God to bear witness to the blood and, by word and by gifts, by prayer, to be fellow-workers with God, that the blood may have the honour which belongs to it. "Not with corruptible things such as silver or gold, but with the precious blood of Christ" will become for them the one all-inclusive thing to which they devote their lives.

A Christian writer (Miss F. R. Havergal) has testified that the insight into what the blood can do in its ever-cleansing power was the beginning of a new experience in her spiritual life. Some time later she wrote: "I see more and more clearly that it is only by the abiding indwelling of the Holy Spirit that this hidden power of the blood can be revealed and experienced." May our lives also be under the teaching of the Holy Spirit that He may constantly keep us also in the heavenly blessedness and joy which the blood has procured for us.

CHAPTER VI

The Blood of the Lamb

" These are they which came out of great tribulation, and have washed their robes, and made them white in the blood of the Lamb." —Rev. vii. 14.

WE have already, in our meditations on the precious blood of Christ, several times considered the question what it really is that bestows such value on the blood. Scripture has given us an answer from more than one viewpoint. It was because of His eternal Godhead, His true manhood, His infinite love, His perfect obedience ; in all these we found a reason why His blood exercised such an immeasurable power with God and men.

The words quoted above call us to the consideration of this subject from still another side.

The new name given here to the blood, " the blood of the Lamb," invites us to inquire what we are specially intended to learn from this expression, and what the peculiar characteristics of the blood and its effects are, which are revealed to us by it and cannot be learned by any other expression than the blood of the Lamb.

When our Lord Jesus is called the Lamb of God there are two leading thoughts which are bound up with that name. One is, that He is the Lamb of God because He was slain as a sacrifice for sin. The other is that He was lamb-like, gentle, and patient. The first emphasises the work that He as a Lamb had to accomplish ; the second emphasises the gentleness which characterised Him as Lamb. The first of these views is the more general one, and we also have often had the opportunity of speaking about the value of the blood from that point of view ; as for instance, in the address on " The altar and the Blood." The second has too often been lost sight of. Let us on this occasion fix our attention specially on it, in order that we may obtain our share of the rich blessing which is contained in it for us. Taking as our point of view the disposition which inspired our Lord as the Lamb of God, we shall see that it is just this which makes the blood so precious—it is the blood of the gentle Lamb of God.

We shall consider what it means, that in heaven they praise the blood as the blood of the Lamb :

I. This Bestows upon the Blood its Value.

II. This Reveals the Nature of Redemption.

III. This Assures us of a Perfect Salvation.

I. The Blood of the Lamb : This Bestows on the Blood its Value.

When Jesus was on earth He said : " Come unto Me . . . Learn of Me, for I am meek and lowly in heart and ye shall find rest unto your souls." He did not mention meekness as one of several other virtues that were to be learned from Him, but as *the* one which was His chief characteristic ; the one that they must learn if they were to find rest for their souls. He who takes the trouble to understand this aright will have a vision of the true inwardness of the work by which our redemption has been obtained.

The Lord came to deliver us from sin. In what does sin really consist ? In self-exaltation ; in pride. This was the sin of the angels who fell. They were created to find their life in God alone. They began to view themselves and the wonderful gifts which God had bestowed upon them with pride : they began to consider that their dependence upon God and subjection to Him were a humiliation, a curtailment of their liberty and enjoyment ; they exalted themselves against God, seeking their own glory instead of that of God. That moment they fell into the abyss of destruction. Pride, self-seeking, changed them from angels into demons; cast them from heaven to hell; turned the light and the blessedness of heaven into the darkness and flames of hell.

When God created a new world with man created for it, to repair the destruction wrought by the fall of the angels, Satan came to lead man into the same opposition to God. The temptation which the serpent presented to the woman was intended simply to draw man away from subjection to God. Along with the words which Satan whispered into Eve's ear, he breathed into her soul the deadly poison of pride. And since man listened to him, self-exaltation became in his case also the root of all sin and sorrow. His life is made up of self-love, self-will, and self-pleasing. Self, " I," is the idol he serves. Self is a thousand-headed monster that, as self-seeking, self-pleasing, self-confidence, self-esteem, is the fruitful mother of all the sin and misery which is to be found in the world.

The authority of Satan is exercised over, the fire of hell burns in, all that belongs to " self," " I," " pride " : and the soul becomes consumed with a thirst that can never be quenched.

If the Lord Jesus were to become our true Saviour one thing was most necessary—He must deliver us from ourselves. He must bring about a death to " self," " I," to the self-life, and lead us again to live for God, so that we may " live no more to ourselves." " No man liveth to himself." This is the only way by which man can become truly blessed. And there is, further, no other means by which this way can be prepared for us, save by the Lord Jesus in His own Person opening the path for us, and obtaining a new life for us, and imparting it to us ; and of that life, denial of self, self-humiliation, should be the chief characteristic and the inner blessedness. So that in this way God might again take up His rightful place and become our All-in-all in that new life.

This is the reason why the Lord Jesus had to come into the

world as the Lamb of God. He had to bring back again to earth the meekness and lowliness of heart in which true submission to God is manifested. It was no longer to be found on earth. He brought it from heaven. In heaven He humbled Himself as Son before the Father, that He might be sent as a servant into the world. He humbled Himself to become man. As man He humbled Himself to the death of the cross. As " the Lamb of God " He denied Himself with a heavenly meekness that surpasses all our thoughts, to become a servant of God and man, that He might please God and man. This was the disposition which inspired Him, and constituted the true nature of His sufferings; which made Him a complete victor over sin. It was as the " Lamb of God " that He took away the sin of the world.

This is what bestows such virtue upon His blood. He inflicted a deadly wound on sin; gaining the victory in His own person. He subjected Himself to the will of God, and through His whole life, under the severest temptations, He sacrificed Himself for the glory of God, with a lowliness and patience and meekness which were the delight of the Father, and of all the holy angels. He did all this as "the Lamb of God." He crowned all this when He shed His blood as " the Lamb of God " for the reconciliation of sin, and for the cleansing of our souls. This is why praise is offered in heaven for His blood, as the blood of " the Lamb of God." This is why the Father has placed Him " in the midst of the throne " as " the Lamb that had been slain." This is why believers, in tender astonishment and love, glorying in the " blood of the Lamb," praise His meekness and lowliness as their greatest joy and their one desire. As " the blood of the Lamb " it possesses virtue and power for complete redemption.

II. This phrase, " The Blood of the Lamb," reveals the true nature of redemption.

The blood has its value because of the disposition of

which it is the token, just as much as its power is manifested in the disposition which it produces. The Lord Jesus came to do in His own person what we could not do, and then to make us, who did not possess it, partakers of the treasure which He had procured. His lowliness is the gift which He brought from heaven; His lowliness is what He wishes to bestow upon us. And as the blood was the manifestation and the result of the divine meekness in Him, so it is also in us the manifestation and result of our contact with the blood.

Our fellowship in His blood, what is it but fellowship in His death? And His death was only the culmination of His humiliation and sacrifice. It was a proof that there was no other way by which to attain to the fullness of the life of God—resurrection life—save through death. And so the blood—as a fellowship in His death; as a participation of the inner power of His death—calls us to give ourselves over to death through His humiliation and self-sacrifice, as the only way to the life of God. A Christian who thinks that he is trusting in the blood, often gives way to pride and self-will and self-exaltation; but if he only really knew that " the blood of the Lamb " is at work in him, every moment, in living power, then he recognises in this fact a decided call coupled with a supply of power, for him, in the meekness of Christ, to manifest his faith in that blood.

This is a subject upon which the attention of Christians must be much more fixed than is generally the case. We must learn that there is no way to heaven save by lowliness, by entirely dying to our pride, and by living entirely in the lowliness of Jesus. Pride is from hell: it is the poison of Satan in our blood; pride must die, or nothing of heaven can live in you. Under the banner of this truth you must surrender yourself to the Spirit of the meek and lowly Lamb, to " the Lamb of God," the victor over all pride.

Each exercise of faith in " the blood of the Lamb," each act of thanksgiving for the love and the blessedness brought to you by it, ought to powerfully encourage you to desire supremely to know and to manifest the humility of " the Lamb of God." All your worship of God from a heart cleansed and saturated by the blood, ought to strengthen you in the blessed certainty that where " the blood of the Lamb " is, there He is Himself in His meekness, to sanctify the heart as a Temple of God.

We must not only recognise that this meek spirit, which in God's sight is of great value, must be the object of our desire and effort; but we must believe that it is really possible for us to obtain a share in it. Jesus Christ is the second Adam, who really restores what the first Adam lost. Our pride and self-seeking, everything that self does or produces, all the sorrow that arises from our self-will and self-love, is only a continuation of that first turning away from God, when Adam fell under the authority of Satan. There can be no thought of any redemption or approach to God without an entire turning back to a life of decided dependence, humility, and submission to God. The only way for redemption from the condition of pride is by death; dying to the life of self, the surrender of the self-life to death, to make room for the new life. And there is nothing in the entire universe that can make that death possible for us, and work out a new life in us, save such a heavenly lowliness as " the Lamb of God " brought from heaven, and which He made transferable to us by His death. What He was when He died, such He was when He arose from the dead. As the " Lamb of God " He is the second Adam, our head, and He lives to bestow His Spirit upon us.

Yes, by His Spirit the Lamb of God will certainly bestow this meekness and will work it out in the heart of everyone who surrenders his life entirely to the power of the blood. We have already seen that the shedding of the blood was followed by the shedding forth of the Spirit, and that the Spirit and the blood bear witness together; where the blood reaches there also the Spirit is. John saw the Lamb in the midst of the throne, standing as if slain, " having seven eyes which are the seven spirits of God sent forth into all the earth " (Rev. v. 6). The Spirit works as the Spirit of the Lamb. He works with a hidden, but divine power, breathing into the heart of His own people that which is the divine glory of the Lamb—His meekness.

Do you desire to understand how these effects of the Blood and the Spirit may be experienced ? Do you complain that you know but little about them ? Do you fear that in you perhaps it may never be possible ? You may learn how it is possible if you are a believer that the Spirit is in you, as a seed of God. That seed appears small and dead ; its life-power is hidden and not yet active. Begin to esteem that seed of the divine nature. Keep calm, that you may quietly believe that the Spirit is in you. Believe that the gentleness of the Lamb is also in you as a seed, a hidden power of the Spirit. Begin in that faith to pray to God to strengthen you by His Spirit in the inner man. Take any hour of the day— say nine o'clock—when you will (even if it is but for one moment) send up a prayer for the bestowment upon you of your inheritance, the meekness and gentleness of the Lamb. Cultivate the disposition of welcoming everything that calls for, or helps you to, humility. You may rely upon it that the hitherto hidden seed, the Spirit of Jesus, will open out and spring up in you, and it will become your experience that the blood of the Lamb has brought you into contact with a lowliness which is powerful and blessed beyond all thought.

III. The Blood of the Lamb—The Assurance of a Perfect Salvation.

We would have thought that in calling our Lord " the Lamb " this name would have been used only in respect to His humiliation in His earthly life. In Scripture it is most used in reference to His glory in heaven. John saw Him stand, as a Lamb that has been slain, in the midst of the throne. The four living creatures, and the four and twenty elders, and the hosts of heaven praise Him as the Lamb who purchased us unto God by His blood. " Salvation to our God and to the Lamb." It is the Lamb who executes judgment, who conquered Satan and all his power. The Lamb is the Temple and the Lamp of the New Jerusalem. It is from beneath the throne of God and of the Lamb that the river of the water of life flows. In heaven, through eternity, the Lamb is all in all. He is the glory and joy of heaven. Eternity will re-echo the song of His praise : " The Lamb that was slain is worthy to receive power and riches and wisdom and strength and honour and glory and blessing."

And why is all this ? " Thou art worthy . . . for Thou wast slain, and hast redeemed us to God by Thy blood " (Rev. iii. 9). It is the blood of the Lamb that bestows this glory upon Him. By His own blood He has entered into the Holy of Holies, and is seated at the right hand of the Majesty in heaven. His blood has accomplished this. Because He humbled Himself to death, therefore God has so highly exalted Him. As " the Lamb of God," meek and lowly of heart, He glorified God even to the pouring out of His life ; therefore He is esteemed to be worthy of being praised for ever by the song of the universe. " Salvation unto our God who sitteth upon the throne, and unto the Lamb." The blood has effected this.

The blood will be effective for us also. All on whom the precious blood has been sprinkled must come to that place where the Lamb is, and where the blood is, where all those who have been bought and cleansed by the blood will honour and praise the Lamb for ever. All on whom the precious blood has been sprinkled will come to the place where the Lamb will lead them to the fountains of living water, and will perfect the salvation which He began in them, as they obtain a share in the marriage supper of the Lamb, and for ever worship God where the Lamb is the Temple and the Light. Yes, certainly the blood of the Lamb is the only, but the certain, pledge of a perfect salvation. And that not only in eternity, but here on earth, in this life. The more we meditate upon the glory of eternity, and listen with amazement to the worship of the Lamb, and contemplate the unspeakable blessedness which He bestows, the more settled will our faith become that the blood which accomplishes such imcomprehensible things there is able to effect here also a heavenly and thought-surpassing power in us.

Yes, the blood of the Lamb that was powerful enough to destroy sin, to open heaven for sinners, and to bring their salvation to such perfection, that blood has surely power to cleanse our hearts, to saturate them, and fill them with all the power and joy which the Lamb on the throne will, even here, pour out upon us.

That blood is powerful to cleanse us from pride, to sanctify us with the holiness of the Lamb, His heavenly gentleness and humility. In Him we see humility crowned by God, and all-conquering gentleness exalted to the throne. He is able to reveal this in our hearts.

The blood of the Lamb : the pledge of a perfect salvation ! Oh, that we in deep astonishment and worship might let our hearts be filled with this truth. Our faith must take time to nourish itself by the reality of what is revealed to us, the reality of what takes place in heaven to-day, and shall continue for ever : the reality of the powerful activities which stream forth from the blood here on earth every moment. In that faith we must present ourselves before Him, who Himself has cleansed us by His blood and made us kings and priests. He Himself will keep alive in us an effective application of the blood. Just as a garment that is to be dyed must be plunged in the liquid which contains the colour, and become saturated by it, so the soul that constantly bathes and cleanses itself in the blood of the Lamb becomes entirely saturated with those dispositions which that blood carries and of which it is full. The gentleness and the humility of the Lamb will

F   [81]

become the adornment of that soul. He Himself will cause us to experience through the blood, as priests, a living entrance to God: an ever-abiding communion with God. He, Himself, will bestow on us, as kings, sovereignty and victory through the blood of the Lamb.

Yes, He Himself will make His blood the pledge of a perfect salvation. Oh, that we might only give glory to the blood of the Lamb! Oh, that each day our heart might sing: "In Jesus' Blood is power"! Oh, that each day our confidence might be: "The blood that is powerful in heaven, is powerful in my heart. The blood that works wonders in heaven, works wonders also in my heart. The blood of the Lamb is my life, my song, my joy, my power, my perfect salvation!" For that blood has come forth from His heavenly gentleness and humility, that blood bestows upon me also the heavenly gentleness and humility through which I enter heaven. The blood of the Lamb: we have learned that it is because it is the "blood of the Lamb" that it has such a divine worth and power. It is the Lamb in His gentleness and humility who has redeemed us; it is gentleness and humility which constitutes the power, the disposition, the inner nature of redemption. It is in the way of gentleness and humility that He sacrificed His own will and life, and died; and so has received a new life from God.

Learn, I pray you, that here is your way to eternal blessedness. Let each contact with the blood be contact with the Lamb; more particularly with His gentleness and meekness. Let your faith touch just the hem of His garment, and power will go out from Him. "Self" is our one sin and sorrow; wholly and always denial of self is our only redemption. Fellowship with the death of the Lamb of God is our only entrance into life that He bestows. If only we knew what a sweet, heavenly, heart-changing power there is in a humility like that of the Lamb of God, which moved Him to give His blood, how this would drive the poison of Satan and pride out of our fallen nature; how this would bestow on us the water of life, to extinguish the fire of our self-seeking ! Would we not rather sacrifice everything, than fail to possess it in full measure ? How we should praise the blood of the Lamb as the revelation, the impartation, and the eternal glory of humility !

CHAPTER VII

" When I See the Blood "

" The blood shall be to you for a token upon the houses where ye are : and when I see the blood, I will pass over you, and the plague shall not be upon you to destroy you, when I smite the land of Egypt . . . "—Exod. xii. 13.

THE story of the passover is well known to us all. The Lord was about to lead His people out of Egypt, and in the night of their departure to inflict judgment upon Egypt. The Lord considered Israel as His firstborn son among the nations. Egypt had transgressed against Him by ill treatment of this firstborn son, and so punishment must fall on " the firstborn " of Egypt. In every house the firstborn would be smitten by the destroying angel, who, at midnight, would pass through the land of Egypt.

The Egyptians and Israelites in many cases dwelt near one another, and so a sign must be set on the door of every Israelitish house, that the destroying angel might not enter there to slay. That sign was to be the blood of a lamb, slain by the father of the family, according to the commandment given by God. " The blood shall be a token to you "—so God had said. It was to be a sign, an assurance by which the Israelite might have entire confidence concerning the safety of his family. It would be a sign also before God, of the disposition of the father of the house, regarding his obedience of faith through which God would spare his house :—" When I see the blood, I will pass over you."

We know why it is that the blood, and nothing else, was established by God as a sign. Although Israel was God's people, they were also, alas, a sinful people. As far as sin was concerned, if it was to be treated as it deserved, then the destroying angel must exercise judgment on Israel also. But the blood was to be a token of redemption. The death of the lamb that was slain was considered as taking the place of the death which man had earned by his sin. The redemption of Israel, however, was not to take place simply by the exercise of power, but according to law and righteousness. Therefore the punishment of the sin of each Israelitish home had to be warded off by the blood of the paschal lamb. Each father of a household, by the sprinkling of blood on the door of his house, had to give proof of his recognition of his sinfulness and need of deliverance; and of his confidence in God's promise of redemption, by his willing obedience to God's command. All this was in a remarkable way represented by the blood of the Paschal lamb.

In the New Testament we read: " Christ, our passover, is sacrificed for us." The outstanding name which He bears in heaven, *viz.* the Lamb of God, refers chiefly to what He, as our paschal lamb, has done for our redemption. And if we wish to declare in the most simple manner how His blood obtains our salvation, then we cannot teach it in a better way than by the type of the Passover in Egypt. Up till now, in explaining the power of Jesus' blood in these chapters we have dealt chiefly with believers. We now address ourselves to the simplest and most unlearned in spiritual things, to those who, as yet, understand nothing about this blood. May God grant to them a knowledge of the preciousness of the blood of Christ by the glorious type supplied by the Passover !

Attention is drawn to :—

I. The Danger to be Averted by the Blood.

II. The Deliverance Effected by the Blood.

III. The Blessings we may Obtain by the Blood.

I. The Danger to be Averted by the Blood.

The danger was (i) awful ; the Eternal God was about to send the destroying angel with his sword through the land.

[85]

It was (ii) general; no house was to be spared. Each family was to be robbed of its crown: the firstborn must die.

(iii) It was certain; no power of man could procure redemption.

(iv) It was unexpected; a terrible picture of the danger that threatens us, and from which there is no deliverance save by the blood of the Lamb.

i. That danger is awful. A hiding-place, a means of redemption, has no value, if danger is not realised. The blood of Jesus, however precious it is in the eyes of God and of the redeemed, has no value for him who has not realised his danger. The world is under the wrath of God. However happily life is spent, however we boast about our present civilization and prosperity and progress, there hangs over this world a heavy, dark cloud, more terrible than that which hung over Egypt. There is a day of judgment approaching, when anger and wrath, tribulation and anguish shall be recompensed to all disobedience and sin. Christ shall appear in flaming fire, taking vengeance on those who "know not God and obey not the Gospel" (2 Thess. i. 8) He will pronounce that terrible sentence upon all who do not belong to Him: "Depart from me, ye cursed, into everlasting fire, prepared for the devil and his angels." Behold the day comes, burning like an oven, and who shall stand when He appears? (Mal. iv. 1).

ii. It was general. No house in Egypt was to be passed by. From the palace of the king to the hut of the beggar, the firstborn had to die. There was no distinction: rich and poor; godless and fashionable; friends and enemies of Israel; innocent children; those who were kind, as well as the most cruel oppressors of the people—that night there was no difference between them. The nation had sinned; the judgment must come upon all, without exception.

It will be just the same with the judgment which is coming upon the world. We all have sinned; we are all under a curse and wrath. No one—unless God Himself in a miraculous manner redeemed him—will escape a judgment which he cannot endure. No reader of these words, whoever he is, can escape standing before God's throne, to be cast into the outer darkness on account of his sins, if God's mercy has not wrought out for him a miracle of grace.

iii. This judgment is certain. We are living in the days of which Scripture has spoken, when scoffers, walking after their own lusts, say: "Where is the promise of His coming, for all things continue as they were from the beginning of the creation." God is longsuffering, and extends the days of grace, but the day of judgment will surely come. No power or force, no wisdom or cunning, no riches or honour can enable man to escape it. It comes certainly. So surely as there is a God in heaven who is a righteous judge, so surely as there is sin on earth opposed to God's holy law, so surely as there is in every child of man consciousness that sin must be punished by a judge, so surely that day will come. Although the thought of the millions who then will be lost, and of the terribleness of the breaking loose of the long pent-up fire of God's wrath, and of the misery of an eternal destruction from God's presence is too terrible to rightly apprehend or bear—it is true and certain. There hangs over the whole world, and over every soul, a dark cloud of the wrath of God, which will speedily break loose and burn with a fire that through eternity will not be extinguished.

iv. The danger is unexpected. In Egypt they were busy buying and selling, building and trading, living delicately and boasting about their power and wisdom, when in one night the whole land was plunged into the deepest sorrow. " And Pharaoh rose up that night, he and all his servants and all the Egyptians, and there was a great cry in Egypt." It was in Egypt, as in the days of the flood, and of Sodom and Gomorrah ; in an hour when they thought not, the angel of destruction came.

It will ever be so. The devil lulls men to sleep by the business and enjoyments of this world: Death comes—

unexpected. Judgment comes—unexpected. While one still puts off to a more convenient season; while another comforts himself with the assurance that he will yet sometime be delivered; while still others do not trouble themselves at all about these things—judgment ever draws nearer. It has happened more than once that a man has fallen asleep on the railway line; everything around him seemed restful and still; suddenly the express train came rushing on, and crushed him to death.

God's judgment draws near with incomprehensible rapidity and power. Because everything around you is quiet and safe and appears joyous, I beseech you, do not deceive yourselves. Judgment comes unexpectedly, and then—then it is for ever too late. Believe this, I pray you, the danger is greater and nearer than you imagine; make haste to be delivered.

II. The Deliverance Effected by the Blood.

i. Deliverance is planned by God Himself. Let this be a settled conviction with you, that no human wisdom is of any avail here. It is from God's judgment, which is so terrible and irresistible, that we must flee. It is God alone who can point out the way of escape. Deliverance by the blood of a lamb was the outcome of divine wisdom, and if a sinner desires to be delivered, then he must learn in this matter to be entirely submissive to God, and entirely dependent upon Him. He must see that he has to deal with what is really a divine purpose, and that, as sure and powerful as the destruction is, just so sure and powerful is the deliverance which has been prepared for him.

ii. Deliverance is through substitution. That was the meaning of the blood of the slaughtered paschal lamb. The Israelite was just as sinful as the Egyptian. If the destroying angel came, he would have the right—yes (if it must go by right) it would be his duty to enter each house of Israel.

But if on the door of the Israelite he found the blood—what does that mean?

When the Israelite took the lamb and raised the knife to slay that innocent creature for the sake of its blood, which he had need of, for his deliverance, he had only one thought in his mind: "I am sinful; my house is sinful; the angel of God's wrath is coming to-night; if He acts according to what I deserve, then death would enter my house; but I offer this lamb to die for me and my house." That word "for me," "in my place" was the one thought in his heart.

This lamb was typical; "God will provide Himself a lamb." He has done this. He has—oh, wonder of wonders!—given His own Son to die in our place. The death which Jesus died was my death. He bore my sins. I need not now die. The deliverance which God has prepared is through substitution. Jesus, my substitute, has paid all—all my indebtedness to God's law, and has done everything for me. He has entirely broken the power of sin and death, and I can now, at once, be entirely acquitted and be freed from all my sins. Deliverance is through substitution.

iii. Deliverance is by means of the sprinkling of blood. The blood of the lamb had to be sprinkled on the door posts. It was not enough that the lamb should be slain and its blood shed; the blood must be personally applied. The father of the family had to take the blood and sprinkle it on the door of his house. And so the Scripture says that our conscience must be cleansed, and our heart must be sprinkled. "Let us draw near . . . having our hearts sprinkled from an evil conscience" (Heb. x. 22).

In this deliverance, God and man meet one another; each has his share in the work. God provided the Lamb—His own Son. God, through the eternal Spirit, prepared Him to be a sacrifice. God promised to accept the blood. God bestows upon us, by the blood, justification, cleansing, and sanctification. All this is the work of God. Our work is to believe in that blood, and in faith to submit ourselves to the sprinkling of it. The result is real and eternal.

iv. Deliverance is through the obedience of faith : for the Israelite it was a new and hitherto unheard-of thing, that the destroying angel was to come, and that the blood on the door would deliver him. But he believed God's word, and in that belief he did what he had been commanded. This is just what you have to do who are longing for deliverance from eternal death. Exercise faith in the blood ; be assured that if God tells you the blood of His Son cleanses you from all sin, that it is the truth. The blood has a supernatural, heavenly, divine power, to cover and blot out sin before God immediately and for ever. Accept this as God's truth, and rest upon it. Then be obedient, and appropriate that blood which accomplishes such wonders. Reckon that it was shed for you ; humble yourself before God, that the Holy Spirit may apply it to you, and cleanse your heart by it. Simply believe in that blood as shed for you. The Almighty God is faithful, and will accept you for the sake of the blood. Jesus will cleanse you by His blood and will work out in you the cleansing, and impart to you the joy and the power which the blood alone can bestow.

v. The blood effects an immediate deliverance from the judgment of God. The blood delivered the Israelites immediately, and entirely, from the threatened danger of that night.

From the moment that you are sprinkled by that blood, you are justified from your sins, and the judgment of God is averted from you. This blessing is so great, so divine, that it appears to man too great to be true, We desire to see in ourselves some token of improvement, to feel something as a proof that God has received us. It seems incredible that God could thus justify the unrighteous immediately, and yet it is so. This is the divine glory of redemption through the blood of the Lamb. That blood has such a divine and life-giving power, that the moment a man believes in it, he is cleansed from all his sins. You who desire to be saved from sin and judgment, may rely upon this. The blood effects an immediate redemption. The blood is so unspeakably precious to God, as the proof of the obedience of His Son, that He, for His sake, and because of His pleasure in Him, immediately forgives and receives you, if only you trust in that blood.

vi. The blood is the beginning of a new life. You know that the Feast of Unleavened Bread was closely connected with the Feast of the Passover. If leaven were used, it came from a portion of the old lump of dough of a previous baking. Leavening is a process of corruption. Israel had to use unleavened bread during the Passover Feast and the seven following days, as a proof that they would no longer have anything to do with the old leaven of Egypt; everything must become entirely new. The sprinkling with the blood of Christ is the commencement of an entirely new life. The blood and the Spirit of Christ are inseparable. When the sinner is brought near to God by the blood, he is renewed and sanctified by the Spirit. The blood is the beginning and pledge of a life in the service of God.

vii. The blood gave assurance of the love and guidance of God. Israel was delivered by the sprinkling of the blood from the power of the destroying angel, and also from the power of Pharaoh. The Red Sea, the pursuit by Pharaoh, and the desert, had still to come, but the blood was the pledge that God would be responsible for everything.

The blood of Christ gives you a share in the love, the guidance, and the protection of God. Oh, if you only understood this—the God who has provided the blood of His Son, who has received you because of that blood—He has become your God. He who has given His Son for you, how shall He not with Him also freely give you all things? This is the blessing and power of the blood—it brings you into an eternal covenant with God; He becomes your leader and your portion.

viii. The blood is the pledge of a perfect redemption.

The God who delivered Israel from Egypt by the blood was not satisfied until He had brought Israel into Canaan. God bestows upon you not only the blood of Christ, but the living Christ Himself. Because He ever lives, He can save to the uttermost. Each moment of your life He will care for you. He undertakes to provide for every weakness and need. He will, here in this life, lead you into the full blessedness of God's love. He becomes surety for your arrival in eternal glory. His blood is the eternal and undeniable proof that all God the Father and Christ see needful They will do, and that They will not forsake you until They have accomplished Their work in you from beginning to end. All the blessedness and all the glory of redemption are securely founded on the precious blood. Oh, you who up till now have had no part in that blood, let me persuade you to seek for salvation in the blood of the Lamb of God. Do not rest until you have the assurance, the perfect certainty, of your redemption.

III. The Blessings we may Obtain by the Blood.

When the Israelite had sprinkled the blood he knew that he was safe. God had given him a promise of protection, and he was able trustfully to await the terrible visit of the destroying angel. He could listen peacefully to the great cry in the streets around him. His safety lay in God, who had said : " When I see the blood, I will pass over you."

How much more may we, who now have not the blood of an earthly lamb, but that of the Lamb of God from heaven—how much more may we be assured of our redemption ? You who read this, give, I pray you, an answer to the question I now ask : Have you this assurance ? Are you truly sheltered from the day of wrath, under the protection of the blood ? Have you the assurance that you also have been redeemed by that blood ? If not, hasten, without delay, to receive this blessing. The danger is so terrible—the redemption is so glorious ;

the conditions are so full of grace; let nothing keep you back from obtaining a share in it. You must be sure about it, or you will have no rest for your soul.

It is recorded that on the Passover night, there was an old grey-haired man who lived in the house of his firstborn son; and he himself was the firstborn son of his father. His son also had a firstborn son. Thus there were three first-born sons in the house, who all must die, if the destroying angel entered the house. The old man was lying on his bed, sick, but he heard with interest everything his son told him about God's command to Moses. Towards evening he was often restless, as he thought of their danger, and he said: "My son, are you sure that you have done everything that has been prescribed?" His answer was: "Yes, father, everything." For a moment he was satisfied. Then he asked again: "Are you sure? Has the blood been sprinkled on the door?" Again the answer was: "Yes, father, everything has been done according to the command." The nearer it came to midnight, the more restless he became. Finally he cried out: "My son, carry me out if you please, that I may myself see it, and then I can rest." The son took his father up, and carried him to where he could see the blood on the side posts, and the lintel. "Now I am satisfied," cried he. "Thank God! Now I know that I am safe!"

My reader, can you say that—"Thank God, now I know that I am safe? I know that the blood was shed for me and has been sprinkled on me?" If not, I beseech you, by the terror and certainty of the judgment of God, make haste this day to hearken to God's word. Turn away from your sin, and place your trust in the blood. Oh! I pray you, add not now to all your other sins, that of despising, rejecting, treading upon, the Blood of the Son of God. I beseech you by the mercy of God, and the wondrous love of the Son of God, flee from the wrath to come, and seek for shelter under the blood which alone can redeem. Believe, I beseech you, that no prayer, no worship, no works, no endeavour, will avail you anything. But God has said: "When I see the blood I will pass over you." Let that be your confidence. If He does not see the blood on me, He will not spare me. Come *now*, to-day, to this dear Saviour, who lives to cleanse you with His blood, and who never once has rejected anyone who came to Him.

CHAPTER VIII

Purchased Unto God by The Blood

" Worthy art Thou . . . for Thou wast slain and hast purchased us to God by Thy blood "—Rev. v. 9.

BOUGHT: that word is understood by everybody. Trading occupies a great place in our lives. We are all so constantly engaged in buying or selling that the ideas attached to it are understood by everybody. The right that the buyer obtains over that which previously had not been his ; the value which he attaches to it after its price has been paid ; the certainty that what he has bought will be given to him ; and the use that he will make of his purchase ; all these things are obvious, and daily, in a thousand ways, they make out the life of the community.

The words of our text, taken from a heavenly hymn of praise : " Thou hast purchased us to God by Thy blood," invite us to see in the mirror of earthly trade, what " the blood of the Lamb " has done for us, and what a clear knowledge of this fact entails. The right that our Lord Jesus, " the Lamb of God," has obtained to us, and the claim that we now have in regard to Him ; what we may expect from Him, what He expects from us—all these things will become plain to us. If the Holy Spirit teaches us to regard the blood in the light of these resemblances, our hearts surely will take up the song of heaven with new joy : " Worthy art Thou . . . for Thou wast slain and hast purchased us to God by Thy blood."

Following these thoughts let us notice :—

    I.   The Right to Us which He has Obtained.

    II.   The Claim He makes upon Us.

    III.   The Joy with which He will Receive Us.

    IV.   The Certainty that He will Preserve and Care for Us.

I. The Right to us which He has Obtained.

"Thou hast purchased us to God by Thy blood"; that indicates to us the right which He has obtained to us. As Creator, the Lord Jesus has a right to every soul of man. Through Him God has bestowed life upon men, that they might be His possession and inheritance. Never on earth has any maker had such a right over his own work as Jesus has over us; we belong to Him.

"It has often happened among men that one has had to buy back what really belonged to him, but had been taken from him by a hostile power. Many times a people has had to buy back their land and freedom by their blood. After that, land and liberty become of increased value."

Thus, the Son of God has ransomed us from the power of Satan. God, at creation, had placed man under the government of His Son. By yielding to the temptations of Satan man fell from God, and became entirely subject to the authority of the Tempter; he became his slave. It was the law of God that prohibited sin and threatened punishment. When man sinned, it was this law that bestowed upon Satan his authority. God had said: "In the day that thou eatest" thou fallest into the power of death. God Himself gave man up to be a slave, in the prison-house of Satan; and for man there was no possibility of redemption save by ransom—by the payment of the price which the law must righteously demand as ransom, for the redemption of prisoners.

You know that word "redemption." In old times when it was the custom that prisoners of war should be made slaves, sometimes a very high price was paid by the friends or rulers of the prisoners as ransom for their deliverance from slavery. Jesus Christ has purchased, with His own blood, our freedom from the prison and slavery of Satan, in which he as our enemy had lodged us, and to which the law of God had condemned us.

[96]

To purchase, to ransom, means always that one valuable thing is given for another. Our souls needed redemption: the law demanded the payment of a ransom. We were under its power and condemnation; we were held as prisoners until what we owed was paid, a recompense for the wrongs we had done—a perfect righteousness. Jesus came and gave Himself in our place: His soul for our soul. He bore our punishment of death, our curse of death; He shed His blood as reconciliation for our sin. That blood was the ransom price by which we are redeemed; He gave His life for our life; His blood gave Him an eternal right to us. And now the message comes to us as from heaven—Jesus has bought us by His blood; He and none else has a right to us. Not Satan, not the world, not ourselves, have any right to us; the Son of God has bought us with His blood: He only has a right to us; we belong to Him.

Oh, my reader, be still and listen, and recognise that right. Perhaps you have never known this, or have never meditated upon it. An eternal price has been paid for you. A price has been paid for you of more value than the whole world—the blood of God's Son. You have been redeemed from the power of Satan; God proclaims you to be now the possession of His Son. And the Son comes to-day to take possession of what belongs to Him. He asks you, " Do you know that you belong to Me ? Will you recognise My right?" His blood, His love, God as judge, the Law as creditor, Satan as gaoler—all agree. The Lord who has redeemed you by His blood, has a right to you. Oh, let your heart respond: " Yes, Lord, I acknowledge that Thou, and Thou alone, hast a right to me."

II. The Claim which He makes upon Us.

" Thou hast purchased us to God by Thy blood." These words remind us of the claim which He makes on us. A person may have a right to something without exercising that right; he lays no claim to it. But it is not thus with Jesus Christ. He comes to us with the urgent request that we should surrender ourselves to Him. You know how, in every ordinary purchase, the buyer has the right to ask that what he has purchased shall be given to him; it is carefully stated when and where the delivery will take place. Jesus Christ sends His servants with the request that without delay, that at the hour, and in the place where the message is delivered, *there* the persons, as His purchased possession, should hand themselves over, and become subject to Him. That message comes to you again to-day. He entreats you to say farewell to all foreign authority that has ruled over you, and to become His sole possession.

Chief among those foreign powers is sin. By our descent from fallen Adam, sin has a terrible, irresistible authority over us. It has soaked to the deepest roots of our nature; it is thoroughly at home in us; it has become our nature. However strongly we may be inclined either by the voice of God, or of conscience, or by the sense of the misery which sin has wrought out in us, or by some desire after good, which may be awakened in us, to forsake the service of sin—sin refuses to release us. As slaves of sin, we have no power to break the bonds which bind us. But Jesus, who has bought us by His blood, now calls upon us to give ourselves to Him. However deeply we experience that we have been sold under sin, and that the law of sin always holds us prisoners, He promises to deliver us from its tyranny, and that He will Himself bestow upon us the power to serve and follow Him as Lord. He asks only for the choice of our hearts, the honest declaration of our will; that we recognise His right and yield ourselves to Him. He will see to it that the authority of sin shall be destroyed.

Another of the foreign powers which has exercised authority over us is the world. The needs and business of the world are so manifold and so urgent; they lay claim to our lives and all our powers. The promises, the enjoyments, the temptations which the world presents to us are so flattering, and exercise such an unconscious influence upon us, that it is impossible for us of ourselves to offer resistance to them. The favour and assistance of the people we associate with, their displeasure and contempt if we separate ourselves from them to live only for God, work out in many an enslavement to the world. It rules over them, and demands their obedience. Satan is the ruler of this world, and through it exercises his power over them. Jesus Christ comes as conqueror of Satan and the world, and asks us to choose which we wish to serve—Him, or this enemy of His. He asks this of us, as those who belong to Him. He points us to His blood, to the right to us which He has obtained, and asks that we should recognise this right and surrender ourselves as His possession.

There is another power, a still stronger one, foreign and hostile to Christ. It is the power of " self." It is here that sin has wrought its most terrible ruin. The doing of our own will, seeking our own pleasure and our own honour, are so deeply rooted in us, that apart from an entire revolution it can never be otherwise. Body and soul, understanding and imagination, inclination and love—all are subject to the terrible power of self-pleasing, to the tyranny of " self." Jesus Christ asks that " self " should be pulled down from the throne, and condemned to death. He asks that in all things His will and not ours should be supreme. He beseeches us to make an end of slavery to other lords, and to give ourselves up to Him as His purchased possession.

Each of us must deal with this claim, this request of " the Lamb of God." How you deal with it will decide what your life will be in time and in eternity. A voice comes to us from heaven, saying : " He is worthy, He has been slain, He has purchased us to God by His blood." Oh, that our hearts might no longer hesitate, but by faith in that divine blood respond to His call and reply : " Thou art worthy,

O Lord! Here I am, take what Thou hast purchased. I yield myself to Thee as Thy possession."

III. The Joy with which He will Receive Us.

"Thou hast purchased us to God by Thy blood"—that gives us the pledge of the joy with which He will receive us. When a sinner has been urged to give himself to the Lord, and he declares his willingness to do so, he is, alas, often hindered by the fear that he is unworthy to be received. He feels himself so sinful, so dead; he feels he is greatly lacking in humility and real earnestness, and in that heartfelt love, which befits one who desires to give himself to such a Lord, that he cannot believe the Lord will receive him so instantly, so fully and so eternally. He cannot understand it, still less does he feel in his heart that it is true.

What a glorious answer to all these questionings is in this word, "Thou hast purchased us to God by Thy blood." Do you not know that if a person buys anything he will surely take possession of it, if it is brought to him? You have, I suppose, sometime bought something? As you have paid your money for it and it was given or brought to you, were you not willing to receive it and take possession of it? The higher the price you paid for it, the less was there any doubt that you would take possession of what you had paid for.

"But"—you will perhaps answer—"if I buy something, I know what it is, and that it is worth the price I paid. But I, with my sinful heart, with everything so dead and miserable—there is reason for me to fear that He who purchased me will not receive me. I am not what I ought to be. When I buy an article and another of less worth is sent to me, I refuse to receive it; I send it back with the message: 'This is not what I bought and for which I have paid.'"

You are right, but consider what the difference is between Him who has bought us by His blood, and human purchasers. He bought what He knew was bad, because it was bad; and which He will accept as bad, that His love may have the joy and glory of making it good. How wonderful this is !—it is nevertheless true ; the worse you are, and the deeper you have sunk in the helplessness of your sin, the more fit you are for Him. The Scripture says : " Christ died for the ungodly ; while we were yet sinners, Christ died for us." It says, further, that the price of Christ's blood was paid for those who denied the Lord, for those who sold Him, even for His rejectors. Understand, I pray you, that Jesus has paid an eternal price for you, as one who is an enemy, as one who is a lawful slave of Satan, as one entirely dead in sin. He comes to you who are in this condition with the request that you will surrender yourself to Him, and with a promise that He will receive you just as you are.

I pray you, do not any longer allow yourself to be kept by Satan from your Lord and Saviour. It is Satan who whispers to you that you are too unworthy, that mercy is not for you because you are so sinful. It is a lie—a lie born in hell. You are *utterly* unworthy, but *not too unworthy* ; for mercy is only for unworthy persons. If you have no desire to serve this Lord, if His love and His blood have no value in your eyes, say so openly, and refuse to give yourself to Him, as His purchased property ; but if your heart acknowledges that you by right belong to Him,—oh, come, I pray you, and believe that He will receive you instantly. And let every doubt depart under the power of that one word : " Thou hast purchased me by Thy blood."

It is impossible for the Lord Jesus to refuse to receive you. Between Him and the Father there is an eternal covenant concerning you. The Father has, righteously, given Him right and authority over you ; He has paid your ransom at the great price that has freed you from the tyranny of Satan. He has been constantly calling you to come to Him. He now entreats you again to give yourself up to Him. How can you be so foolish as to think that He will not receive you ? Then doubt no longer. Although you are devoid of feeling, and everything appears cold and dead, come and cast yourself down before Him, and say to Him that as He has bought you, you rely upon Him to receive you. He will certainly do so.

IV. The Certainty that He will Protect us and Care for Us.

"Thou hast purchased us to God by Thy blood." This assures us that He will preserve us and care for us. The man who has purchased something of value, for instance a good horse, not only receives it when it is brought to him, but he appreciates it, he takes care of it, and provides for it. He exercises it and he uses it. He does all this that he may have the utmost service and pleasure out of it. When Jesus Christ receives us—however glorious that is—it is only the beginning. We can rely on Him who bought us by His blood to complete His work in us.

It is just the want of insight into this truth that holds many troubled persons back from surrender, and causes many of weak faith to live always in trouble and worry. They do not apply to spiritual things what they understand so well in earthly affairs. When a man has paid a high price for something, even if only a horse or a sheep, he takes it for granted that he must care for it, in order that he may have pleasure and service from it. And the Lord Jesus—how is it that you do not understand it?—takes upon Himself to care for you, and so to order things that He may attain His purpose in you. You cannot guard yourself against temptation or going astray. You cannot manage yourself or make yourself fit for His service. You cannot direct yourself so that you may know how to act in everything according to His will and that of the Father. You cannot do it. But He can; He will, as the One who has bought you with His blood.

My fellow-believer, the right that the Lord Jesus has obtained to you is so infinitely high, so broad, so unlimited, that if you will only think about it, you will respond to it. Just as I desire that every member of my body—the eye, the ear, the hand, the foot—should always be at my service, so the Lord desires that you, as a member of His body, along with every power and faculty, should always, without a moment's break, serve Him. You are so far from being able to do this that you do not even apprehend it. Cease trying to do it, and begin each day by committing yourself to the almighty preservation and control of your Lord. Just as a horse or a sheep with each new day must be afresh cared for by its owner, even more so must you, as the property of the Son of God, be cared for by Him. Christ is not an owner who is *outside* of you, or who is only in heaven above; He is *your Head*, and just as the first Adam lives within you with his sinful nature, so He, as the second Adam, *lives in you* with His holy nature and by His Holy Spirit. And the one thing to which He calls you, is to trust Him, to wait on Him, to confidently rely upon Him; to finish in the outward things of our lives, His hidden and unnoticed work of protection and perfection. Would that each one of us might know what is implied by our being accepted as the blood-bought possession of Jesus. It implies:

i. That He has set a very high value upon us, and so He will not allow any evil to befall us. He will manifest His love to us; He has need of us for His work and glory, and it is His desire and joy to adorn us with His salvation, and to fill us with His unspeakable joy. Meditate upon this till it becomes fixed firmly in your mind.

ii. That our great need is to recognise ourselves as His possession, and by a reverent confession of this, to have the heart filled by the consciousness of it. Just as a faithful dog often shows so great an attachment to his owner that he will not cease following him, let the wonderful ownership of Jesus, His blood-bought right, so possess you that it will every moment be the key-note of your life, and the power of an enduring attachment to Him.

iii. That we should cultivate trust in Him, and let it completely control our whole soul and every thought as to how we are to spend our life and do our work. A possession is preserved and cared for by the owner. Jesus, my heavenly and almighty Owner, who has bought me for Himself by His blood, and prizes me as " the dear purchase " of that blood, He will surely protect me, He will surely fit me for all things in which He intends to make use of me.

" Thou art worthy, for Thou wast slain, and hast redeemed us to God by Thy blood." Oh, my readers, listen, I pray you, to the song of heaven, and let it begin to sound in your heart. Let it be the heart confession of your relationship to the slain Lamb. Remember, I pray you, that the blood is the power of salvation, and the subject of heavenly praise. Remember that the blood is the power that binds us to Jesus in bonds that cannot be loosened.

Let him who has not yet acknowledged the claim of Christ do so to-day, and let him now say : " Thou art worthy ; for the sake of Thy blood Thou shalt have me."

Let him who has already acknowledged the Lord's claim abandon himself to the heavenly influences of the Holy Spirit for the destruction of all doubt and slowness of heart, and for the enduement of power to live wholly for " the Lamb of God."

Meditate upon and adore God for this divine wonder, that you have been bought by the blood of the Son of God, and let your life become a translation into earthly walk and behaviour of the song : " Thou art worthy, for Thou wast slain, and hast purchased us to God by Thy blood."

CHAPTER IX

The Sprinkling of Blood, and the Trinity

" Peter . . . to . . . the elect according to the foreknowledge of God the Father, in sanctification of the Spirit unto obedience and the sprinkling of the blood of Jesus Christ : grace unto you, and peace, be multiplied."—1 Peter i. 1, 2.

THE Tri-unity of the Godhead is often considered as merely a matter of doctrine, and having no close relationship to the Christian life.

This is not the view of the New Testament, when it describes the work of redemption, or the idea of the life of God. In the Epistles the three Persons are constantly named together, so that in each activity of grace all three together have a share in it. God is triune ; but in everything that He does, and at all times, the Three are One. This is in entire agreement with what we see in nature. A trinity is found in everything. There is the hidden, inner nature ; the outward form ; and the effect. It is not otherwise in the Godhead. The Father is the eternal being—I AM—the hidden foundation of all things, and fountain of all life. The Son is the outward form, the express image, the revelation of God. The Spirit is the executive power of the Godhead. The nature of the hidden unity is revealed and made known in the Son, and that is imparted to us and is experienced by us through the agency of the Spirit. In all Their activities the Three are inseparably One.

Everything is *of* the Father, everything is *in* the Son, everything is *through* the Spirit.

In the words of our text, which Peter writes to believers to whom also he sends his greetings, we find the relationship in which each redeemed one stands to the three persons of the Godhead is clearly set forth.

i. They are elect " according to the foreknowledge of

God." The source of our redemption is in the counsel of God.

ii. They are chosen " in sanctification of the Spirit " : the entire carrying out of the counsel of God is through the Holy Spirit, and the sanctification and the impartation of divine holiness which He works.

iii. They are elect " to obedience and the sprinkling of the blood of Jesus Christ " : the final purpose of God is the restoration of man to a state where the will of God will be done on earth, as it is done in heaven, and where everything will redound to the glory of the free grace which has been revealed so gloriously in the death and blood of the Son of God.

The place which " the sprinkling of blood " takes is most remarkable. It is mentioned last, as the great final end, in which, according to the foreknowledge of the Father, the sanctification of the Spirit, and submission to the obedience of Christ, it finds completion.

In order that we may understand its place and worth in redemption, let us consider it in the light of :

I.   The Glorious Purpose of the Triune God.

II. The Mighty Power by which that Purpose was Attained.

III. The Counsel in which Everything Originated.

I.   The Purpose of the Triune God.

Christians are described as " elect unto . . . obedience and the sprinkling of the blood of Jesus Christ." In the Holy Trinity the place occupied by the Lord Jesus is characterised by the name which He bore as " the only-begotten Son of God." He is literally and really the only One with whom God the Father can or will have anything to do. As the Son, He is the mediator through whom God wrought in creation, and by whom the creature can draw near to God.

God dwells in the hidden and unapproachable light of a consuming fire : Christ is the Light of Lights, the light in which we can view and enjoy the Deity. And the eternal election of God can have no higher purpose than to give us a share in Christ, and through Him, approach to the Father Himself.

Because of sin there was no possibility for man again to be brought near to God, save through reconciliation, by means of the sprinkling of the blood of Christ. Scripture speaks of Him as the " Lamb slain before the foundation of the world." It is stated that we are elect . . . to the sprinkling of the blood of Christ, which means that God ever and always saw that the only way by which salvation could be made possible for us, the only needful thing by which the door of Heaven could be opened for us, and the right and fitness procured for us to obtain a share in all the blessings of His love, was by the sprinkling of the blood. And it tells us further that when the blood occupies the place in our eyes and hearts that it occupies in the eye and heart of God, we shall then certainly enter into the full enjoyment of what He has acquired for us by it.

What these blessings are is clearly revealed to us in the Word of God. " You who were afar off have been brought nigh through the blood." " We have liberty to enter into the most holy place through the blood." " He has cleansed us from our sins by His blood." " How much more shall the blood of Christ purge your conscience to serve the Living God." " The blood of Jesus Christ cleanses from all sin." Many such statements show us that the cleansing and fitness to draw near to God, that the true and living entrance into fellowship with Him, is the blessed effect of " the sprinkling of blood " on our heart and con-science. In the depths of eternity that blood of sprinkling was the object of the unspeakable good pleasure of the Father, as the means of the redemption of His elect. Is it not obvious that when that blood becomes the good pleasure and joy of a sinner, and he seeks life and salvation in that blood, then the heart of God and the heart of the sinner meet one another, and an inner agreement and fellowship, which nothing can break, is found in the blood? The Father has elected us to the sprinkling of the blood, that we may heartily accept of it, and find our entire salvation in it.

There is still another word to consider: elect to obedience and the sprinkling of the blood of Jesus Christ. Here the two sides of the life of grace are placed together for us in a most striking way. In "the sprinkling of blood" we learn what Christ has done *for*, and *to* us; in "obedience" we have what is expected *from* us. The creature can have no other blessedness than that found in the will of God, and in the doing of it as it is done in heaven. The Fall was simply the turning away of man from God's will, to do his own will. Jesus came to alter this, and to bring us again into obedience; and God lets us know that He, in His eternal choice, had these two things in view: "obedience" and "the sprinkling of the blood." The placing together of these two words teaches us the very important lesson that obedience and the sprinkling of blood are inseparably united. It was so with the Lord Jesus. Apart from His obedience, the shedding of His blood would have been of no value. The blood is the life; life consists of disposition and will. The power of Jesus' blood lies wholly in this, that He offered Himself without spot to God, to do His will, subjecting His own will utterly to the will of God. "He became obedient unto death, *therefore* God hath highly exalted Him." He who receives the blood of Jesus receives with it, as his life, His disposition of utter obedience to God. "Obedience and the sprinkling of the blood" are inseparably bound together. The disposition manifested by Christ, in the shedding of His blood, must become the disposition of those on whom it has been sprinkled.

He who desires to have the benefit of the blood must first submit himself to an obedience of faith, which must characterise his whole life. He must understand that " the blood " is constantly crying out : " God's will must be done, even to death." He who truly experiences the power of the blood of Jesus will manifest it by a life of obedience. In the heart of God, in the life and death of Christ, in the heart and life of the true Christian, these two things will always go together.

If any Christian asks why it is that he enjoys so little of the peace and cleansing of the blood, he may be almost certain that the reason is that he has not fully surrendered himself to be obedient. If anyone asks how he may obtain the full enjoyment of the power of the blood—the reply may be :—" Set yourself resolutely to obey God. Let your motto be : ' My will in nothing—God's will in everything ' ; that is what the blood of your Redeemer teaches you." Do not separate what God from the beginning has joined together—obedience and the sprinkling of the blood—and you will thus be led into the fullness of blessing. From eternity God has elected you to both obedience and the sprinkling of the blood.

It may be that you shrink from this demand. Such obedience seems to you to be out of your reach, and as you hear about the power and blessedness obtainable by the sprinkling of the blood, even that seems to you to be out of reach. Do not be discouraged, but attend to what has yet to be said.

II.   The Mighty Power by which that Purpose was Attained.

The Holy Spirit is the great power of God. In the Holy Trinity He proceeds from the Father and the Son. He, by His omnipotent but hidden activity, executes the divine purpose ; He reveals and makes known the Father and the Son. In the New Testament the word " Holy " is applied to Him more often than to the Father or the Son, and He is almost always called " the Holy Spirit " because it is He who from the inward being of God transfers holiness to the Redeemed. The life of God is where His holiness dwells. Where the Holy Spirit imparts the Life of God, there He imparts and maintains the holiness of God, and thus is called the Spirit of sanctification. So the text says that we are " elect to obedience and the sprinkling of the blood of Christ by the sanctification of the Spirit." It is committed to the Holy Spirit by His holy power to watch over us, and to fulfil God's purpose in us. Elect in sanctification of the Spirit unto obedience.

The Spirit of sanctification and obedience: these two go together in the purpose of God. Here we have also a solution to the difficulty already mentioned, that it is not possible for us to render the obedience that God demands. Because God knew this much better than we do, He has made provision for it. He bestows upon us the Spirit of sanctification, who so renews our heart and inward nature, and fills us with His holy and heavenly power that it becomes really possible for us to be obedient. The one needful thing is that we should recognise and trust in the indwelling of the Holy Spirit, and follow His leading.

His inward activity is so gentle and hidden; He unites Himself so entirely with us and our endeavours, that we still imagine that it is our own thinking or willing, where He has already been the hidden Worker. Through this disregard of Him we cannot believe that when we have a conviction of sin, or a willingness to obey (both the result of His inward activity), that He has also power to perfect that work in us. Let him therefore, who really desires to be obedient, be careful persistently and quietly to maintain this attitude of trustful confidence: " The Spirit of God is in me "; and let him bow reverently before God with the prayer that He would " strengthen him with His Spirit, by power, in the inner man."

In sanctification of the Spirit: this supplies the power which enables us to be obedient, and through which also we experience what the sprinkling of the blood means and imparts.

This is the reason why so many of God's people have to complain that after all they have learned, and heard, and thought, and believed about the blood, they experience so little of its power. This is not to be wondered at, for that learning, and hearing, and thinking, and believing, is in a great part only a work of the understanding. And even when prayer is made for the Holy Spirit, it is all in expectation that He will give us clearer *ideas* of the truth. No—this is not the way. The Spirit dwells in the heart: it is there He desires to do His first and greatest work. The heart must first be made right, and then the understanding will lay hold of the truth, not merely as a mental idea, but will preserve it within his Christian life. We are chosen in sanctification of the Spirit—not in the activities of the understanding— to the sprinkling of the blood.

Everyone who desires to know the power of the blood of Jesus must remember that the Spirit and the Blood bear witness together. It was by the shedding of the blood, and by the sprinkling of that blood before God in heaven, that the Spirit was free to come and dwell among us, and in us. It was to assure the hearts of the disciples concerning the glorious and powerful effect of the blood in heaven, in opening a free and bold entrance to God ; and to make them partakers of the blessedness and power of the heavenly life that was now their portion, that the Holy Spirit was sent into their hearts. The first Pentecost, in all its power and blessing, is our portion also ; our inheritance. Would that we might cease to seek in our own strength salvation and blessings purchased for us by the blood. If only we began to live as those who have been led in sanctification of the Spirit to the full experience of what the blood can do, we should have, as never before, a real entrance into an eternal abiding-place near God, and fellowship with Him. We should know what it is to have a conscience cleansed by the blood, " to have no more conscience of sin," to have the heart entirely cleansed from an evil conscience, and so have liberty for an abiding intercourse with God. The Holy Spirit, as we commit ourselves to His leading, is able, in a moment, to bring us into that relationship to Him, in which we shall expect everything from Him.

We have seen what is the work of the Son, and of the Spirit; let us now ascend to see the place which the Father occupies.

III. The Counsel in which Everything Originated.

Peter writes to " the elect according to the foreknowledge of the Father, in sanctification of the Spirit, to obedience and the sprinkling of the blood of Jesus Christ." The counsel of the Father is the origin of everything : and that in the Godhead as well as in the work of redemption. In the Godhead the Son proceeds from the Father, and the Spirit from the Father and the Son. The whole counsel of redemption is also solely " according to the purpose of Him who worketh all things after the counsel of His own will " (Eph. i. 11). From the greatest—the ordering of the work of the Son and of the Holy Spirit—to the least—the conclusion of each dispensation in the history of His kingdom, with all occurrences in it, and the choice of those who will obtain a share in it—all this is the work of the Father. Sanctification of the Spirit, obedience, and the sprinkling of the blood, is the portion of the elect, according to the foreknowledge of the Father.

Scripture, without contradiction, teaches an eternal election. That this teaching should be strongly opposed, is because it is a divine mystery beyond human comprehension. That it has an *appearance* of unrighteousness, can be admitted. That it leads to conclusions which seem strange and terrible to our understanding, we do not deny. To comprehend it, man would need the omniscience and the wisdom of Him who sits upon the throne. And to take up our place on the throne, and give our judgment upon the eternal portion of mankind—may we be preserved from that! Our place is at the footstool of the throne, in deepest reverence; believing what God says, and adoring Him whose doings surpass all our thoughts.

Our text calls us not to reason about these hidden mysteries, but to rejoice, if we are believers, in what is revealed to us in it, and to make a practical use of it. And then this truth calls us to take special notice of the sure ground in which our expectation of salvation is rooted. The sprinkling of the blood, with the obedience which accompanies it, and the sanctification of the Spirit by which both of these reach their full authority over us—all these things are from God.

You may, with the most entire confidence, reckon that He who has thought out this wonderful counsel so far and gloriously carried it out in the sprinkling of the blood in heaven, and the sending of the Spirit from heaven, will just as surely and gloriously carry it out in your soul. This is the right use of the doctrine of predestination—leading you to cast yourself down before God, and to acknowledge that from Him, and through Him, and to Him are all things; and to expect everything from Him alone. Take your place before God, my fellow-believer, in deep reverence and complete dependence. Do not imagine that now God has revealed Himself in Christ and by the Spirit, that you, by making use of what you have learned from this revelation, can work out your own salvation. Let it not be thought of! God must work in you to will and to do, before you can work it out. God must work in you by the Spirit, and by Him must reveal Christ in you. Give God the glory, and let the fullest dependence upon Him be the key-note of your life of faith. If God does not do everything in you, all is in vain. If you expect anything from yourself, you will receive nothing; if you expect all from God, God will do everything in you. Let your expectation be from God alone.

Apply this to all upon which we have been meditating concerning obedience. "Elect unto obedience"; how certain then it is that obedience is indispensable, that it is possible, that in it lies the salvation of God. The Son was obedient unto death. But this was because He had said: "The Son can do nothing of Himself." He submitted Himself to the Father in order that *He* might do everything in Him. Let every desire to do the will of God, every fear of your own weakness, drive you to Him who has elected you to obedience. Predestinated to obedience: that gives assurance that you can be obedient. God Himself will accomplish His purpose in you. Become nothing before Him; He will become all.

Apply it especially to the blessed "sprinkling of the blood" of Jesus Christ. It was this that led us to the choice of this text. Your heart is longing with great desire—is it not?—to live every day under the clear consciousness: "I have been sprinkled with the eternal, precious, divine blood of the Lamb." Your heart longs after all the blessed effects of that blood, redemption, pardon, peace, cleansing, sanctification, drawing near to God, joy, victory—all of which come through the blood. Your heart longs to experience constantly these blessings in full measure. Cast fear aside—you have been elected by God to the sprinkling of the blood of Christ Jesus; you must steadfastly rely on the fact that God, as God, will bestow it upon you. Wait continually upon Him in patience of soul, and confidently expect it. He "works all things according to the counsel of His own will"; He Himself will surely work it out in you.

Apply this also to the sanctification of the Spirit. He is the link that binds together the middle and the end; His is the power that brings together the eternal purpose of God, and a life of obedience and the sprinkling of the blood. Do you feel that this is the one thing that you desire and for which you must wait, that you may inherit the full blessing? Understand that it is God Himself who bestows the Spirit;

who works through the Spirit; who will fill you by the Spirit. How can God who elected you " in sanctification of the Spirit" allow you to lack that without which His purpose cannot be carried out? Be confident about this; ask and expect it with utter boldness. It is possible to live in the sanctification of the Spirit, because it has been designed for you from eternity.

The sprinkling of the blood is the light or revelation of the Trinity—how wonderful and glorious it is! The Father designed the sprinkling of the blood and elected us to it; the Son shed His blood and bestows it on the obedient from heaven; the Spirit of Sanctification makes it our own, with abiding power, and imparts to us all the blessings which He has obtained for us. Blessed sprinkling of the blood! Revelation of the triune God! May this be our joy and our life each day.

CHAPTER X

Washed in His Blood

" To Him that loved us, and washed us from our sins in His own blood, and has made us kings and priests unto God His Father, to Him be glory and power for ever and ever, Amen."—Rev. i. 5, 6.

THE Apostle John dwelt in spirit before the doors of an open heaven when he was in Patmos. Time after time he saw in divine visions the glory of God, and of the Lamb, and of the Redeemed. Of all the things which he saw, the most wonderful was that which caused the four living creatures, and the four and twenty elders, and the angels, and the redeemed and the whole creation, to fall down repeatedly in ecstasy and adoration—the vision of the Lamb standing as it had been slain, in the midst of the throne. And of everything which he heard, that which most deeply impressed him was the frequent mention made in heaven of the blood of the Lamb. In the hymn of praise of the redeemed he had heard the words : " Thou art worthy, for Thou wast slain, and hast purchased us to God by Thy blood." And in the reply of the elder to the question to which John could give no answer, he offered this explanation : " These are they who have washed their robes, and made them white in the blood of the Lamb."

John had been commanded to describe what he had seen and heard. He commences his Book (Rev. i. 4–6) by a greeting similar to those we find in the Epistles—" Grace to you, and peace, from Him which is, and which was, and which is to come "—the Eternal God. Then he mentions the Spirit : " and from the seven Spirits which are before the throne " ; and then follow these words : " and from Jesus Christ "—as he had seen Him—" the firstborn from among the dead, the Prince of the kings of the earth."

The mention of the name of the Lord filled John's heart

with joy and praise, and impressed by what he had heard in heaven, he cried out : " To Him who loved us, and washed us from our sins in His own blood, and hath made us kings and priests—to Him be the glory and the power for ever and ever, Amen."

It is the blood, and being washed in that blood, which is the central point in his praise. So glorious and so heavenly did this blessing seem to him, coupled as it was with the love whence it sprang and the salvation into which it leads, that his heart, set on fire with heavenly zeal, cried out : " To Him be glory and power for ever."

We have for some time been meditating upon the blood of Jesus. If there is one thing that befits us, which would be a proof that we have recognised something of the glory and power of that blood, it would be that we also, as we think of it, cry out : " To Him be the glory for ever and ever."

We shall consider John's song of praise. May it be granted to us to see something of what he saw, to feel something of what he felt, to receive something of the fire which inspired him, and to bring something of the offering of praise that he brought. Let us to that end fix our attention on the place which the blood occupies in this thanksgiving, and enquire what it means that :—

    I.   He has Washed us in His Blood.

    II.   He has made us Kings and Priests.

    III. He Loved Us.

    IV. Glory is Ascribed to Him for Ever for These Things.

I. He has Washed us in His Blood.

We know what the word " washing " means. We wash out bodies to cleanse them from the least defilement that adheres to us. Our clothes are washed to remove every stain or spot. Now, sin is not merely a transgression of the law of God which is reckoned to us as guilt from which we must obtain acquittal or pardon. Sin has an effect upon our souls. It is a pollution which cleaves to us. The blood of Jesus procures for us more than the pardon for our guilt. When this has been powerfully brought to our hearts by the Holy Spirit—then at the same time the blood manifests its cleansing efficacy, so that our souls, in the consciousness of the power of a full deliverance from the sense of defilement in God's sight, know that they have been washed whiter than snow.

John speaks of this two-fold work of grace in his first Epistle. He writes : " If we confess our sins, He is faithful and just to forgive us our sins and to cleanse us from all unrighteousness." To the same effect he had previously said : " If we walk in the light as He is in the light "—that is in the pardoning and sanctifying love of God—" we have fellowship one with another and the blood of Jesus Christ His Son cleanseth us from all sin " (1 John i). This refers to the abiding and uninterrupted cleansing of sin in the case of him who walks in the light, in fellowship with God.

Where does this washing take place, and what is it really that is washed ? It is the heart. It is in the deep, hidden, inner life of man that this effect of the blood is experienced. Jesus said : " The Kingdom of God is within you." Sin has penetrated into the heart, and the whole nature has become saturated with it. The blood too must penetrate the heart ; as deeply as the power of sin has gone, so deeply must the inner being be cleansed by the blood. We know that when some article of clothing is washed, the water with its cleansing power must soak in as deeply as the stain, if it is to be removed. Even so must the blood of Jesus penetrate to the deepest roots of our being : our heart, our entire personality must be reached by the cleansing power of the blood. " The blood cleanses from all sin " ; where sin has reached, there too must the blood follow it ;

where sin ruled, there the blood must rule : the entire heart must be cleansed by the blood. However great may be the depth of the heart, however manifold and lively its activities may be, the blood is just as wonderful and penetrating in its effects. It is in our hearts that the cleansing by the blood of Jesus must take place.

We are told : " They have washed their robes, and made them white in the blood of the Lamb."

A person's position or character can often be told by his clothing. Royal robes are a sign of royal estate. Filthy or torn garments are a sign of poverty or carelessness. " White Robes " indicate a holy character. Thus we read of the Lamb's Bride . . . " To her it was granted that she should be arrayed in fine linen, clean and white : for the fine linen is the righteousness of the saints " (" righteousness " here is the translation of a word which means " the righteous acts," Rev. xix. 8).

The message of the Lord Jesus to the Church at Sardis was : " Thou hast a few names even in Sardis which have not defiled their garments, and they shall walk with me in white, for they are worthy " (Rev. iii. 4).

Out of the heart " are the issues of life "—just in proportion as the heart is cleansed, so the entire life is cleansed, the whole man inwardly and outwardly is cleansed by the power of the blood.

How is this washing effected ? It is done by our Lord Jesus Himself " who washed us from our sins in His own blood." The washing began in an act personally accomplished in us by our Lord. He alone can perfect the work which He carries on in us by the Holy Spirit. Sin invaded our lives : our powers of thought, will, and feeling were all brought under its authority, and this was not an authority exercised from without, or occasionally, but one which was so united with these powers of ours that they themselves became altogether sinful. But now the Holy Spirit takes possession of the place in which sin had become entrenched.

"The Spirit is life," and He becomes the life of our lives. Through Him the Lord Jesus carries on His work in us. Through Him also the blood is constantly applied in its cleansing power.

Our Lord is a High Priest "in the power of an endless life," and thus the cleansing power of the blood of the Son of God is unceasingly conveyed to us. As we wash and cleanse ourselves daily, and thus are refreshed and invigorated, so the Lord bestows upon the soul which trusts in Him the enjoyment of a constant sense of cleansing by the blood. It is He Himself who cleanses us from sin, while we on our part receive the cleansing by faith, by that faith through which at first we receive the pardon of sin. But faith's capacity is now enlarged by obtaining a spiritual view of the divine power and continuous activity of the blood. By this insight faith obtains a spiritual understanding, and becomes able to apprehend the fact that just as the blood has had an infinite effect in the Holiest in heaven, so sin has been completely and finally atoned for before God; it has just as great efficacy in the temple of our hearts to cleanse them entirely. Faith beholds the Lord Jesus, the great High Priest, living in the heart. He cleanses it in the blood which ever retains its efficacy. Faith has learned that full salvation consists in one thing—Jesus Himself who has cleansed us by His blood is our *life*.

II. Who has made us Kings and Priests unto God and His Father.

This is the position for which we are prepared and to which we are exalted by the cleansing of the blood. In this the power of the blood is manifested. If we wish to apprehend aright the spiritual connection between these two positions which are ours through the blood, we must learn it from the experience of the Lord Jesus Himself.

It was only after He had shed His blood that He was

able to enter the Holiest as Priest, and to ascend the throne as King. It was His blood which conquered sin, and by it He was consecrated to enter into the Holiest, into God's presence as Priest, and the blood bestowed on Him the right, as Victor, to rule as King in the glory of God. Such is the heavenly and divine power which the blood possesses.

Now, when the blood comes into contact with us and we by faith recognise its full power, it produces in us also the disposition and fitness to become priests and kings. As long as we think that forgiveness of sins is all that is to be obtained by the blood, we shall neither understand what the Kingly Priesthood means, nor shall we have any desire for it. But when the Holy Spirit teaches and enables us to believe that the blood can accomplish in us also what it accomplished in the Lord Jesus personally, then the heart is opened to receive this glorious truth ; the blood opens the way into a kingly priesthood. It was so to the Lord Jesus, it may be so with us also.

Let us no longer be content with standing still at the beginning of things, but let us press on to perfection—to the knowledge of the perfection prepared for us in the Lord Jesus—entrance by His power into the life in the Holiest ; into a fellowship in the life of Jesus, our Priestly King.

What now does it mean that He, when He has cleansed us by His blood, also makes us priests and kings to God and His Father ? The principal idea attached to the title " king " is that of authority and rule ; to the title " Priest " that of purity and nearness to God. The blood of Jesus constitutes us priests, and gives us admission into the presence, the love, and the fellowship of God. We are so cleansed by the blood as to be fitted for this. Jesus so fills us with His Spirit, with Himself, that we in Him may truly draw near to God as Priests.

The blood of Jesus carries in it so much of His victory over sin and death, that it inspires us with the consciousness of His victorious power, and bestows upon us victory over

[121]

sin and every enemy. He makes us kings. Jesus, the living, Priestly King on the Throne, cannot manifest in us His full power by exercising it from above, or from the outside, but only by indwelling. When He, the Priestly King, takes up His abode within us, He makes us kings and priests.

Do we wish to know the purpose of this? The answer is not far to seek. Why is Jesus seated as a Priest on the throne of the heavens? It is that man may be blessed, and that God may be glorified in man. As Priest He lives only for others, to bring them near to God. He lives as King only that He might reveal the kingdom of God in us and through us. He makes us priests that we might serve the living God; that we might bring others near to Him; that we might be filled with His Spirit so as to be a blessing to others.

As priests through the blood of Christ we live for others, to pray for them; to work among them; to teach them; to bring them to God. To be a priest is no idle self-seeking blessedness. It is a compelling power to enter into God's presence on behalf of others; the power to pray for blessings. and to receive and carry and distribute them. He makes us kings to complete and perfect the priesthood. It is because of this the idea of authority stands out so prominently. Jesus fills us with a kingly disposition; He enables us to rule over sin, over the world, over men. In the midst of all circumstances and difficulties, of all opposition or cruelty, the Christian who yields himself to be made king by Christ lives in the joyous certainty that he is one with Him who has won the victory, and that he in Him is more than conqueror.

III. Who Loved Us.

We have spoken of the blood in which Jesus has cleansed us, and of the glory to which He has exalted us. Let us now ascend to the fountain-head from which all this flows out to us—it is He loved us. If we desire to really understand the salvation which God bestows upon us—to understand it so that it will tune our voices to sing like that of John, "to Him be the glory"—we must first of all understand that its origin and power are in the love of Jesus. Love is the greatest glory of salvation; as it springs from love as its source, it must lead us to that love as its object and nature. Love always suggests a personal, mutual attachment. This is the most wonderful thing in salvation, and it is almost impossible to lay hold of—that the Lord Jesus desires to honour us with His love and His friendship. He wishes to have fellowship with us as His loved ones, and to fill and satisfy our hearts with His divine love.

It is John specially who teaches us what this love is. In his Gospel he tells us the Lord Jesus Christ said that as the Father loved Him, so He also loved us. Our Lord was one with the Father in nature and life. It is difficult for us to form any idea of what that unity is; but love, as the revelation of this unity, helps us in some small measure to understand it.

In love the Father goes out of Himself and communicates Himself to the Son, in whom is His delight and life. He imparts to the Son all He has, and holds communion with Him in a life of giving and receiving. The Father has no life nor delight nor pleasure apart from the Son. That is the love wherewith Jesus loves His own. He gave Himself for them; imparts Himself to them; lives in them. He wishes to have no life apart from them. From the beginning of His love, in pitying them and sympathising with them, He passed on to the love of good pleasure and fellowship, with a view to a unity in which they would dwell in Him and He in them; His desire and rest was in them, and they learned "with all saints to apprehend something of a love which passeth understanding." Only the Holy Spirit can lead the soul personally into that love. "The love of God is shed abroad in our hearts by the Holy Spirit who is given unto us."

The love of God is such a supernatural, heavenly power,

we might perhaps make it a matter of thought, and by that means create some impression in our hearts—but a real participation in it from heaven is such a divine matter that none but those who have with great tenderness and whole-heartedness yielded themselves to be led and taught by the Holy Spirit can come to the knowledge of it. The love of God is plainly declared in Scripture to be the result of Christ dwelling in the heart. Only where the inner inter-course with the Lord has become in a measure the joy and experience of every day can we know what the Lord meant when He said: "Continue ye in My love." "To him that loved us and washed us from our sins in His own blood, and made us kings and priests unto God and His Father." Let us consider Jesus as He was when as man He suffered and died for us, to give His blood for us. Let us allow Him to reveal in us the meaning and heavenly power of that blood. He will teach us that the most glorious fact in all His work is that it is the gift and bearer of His eternal, unceasing love toward us. Let us think of whither He is carrying us— it is to a full partnership in His Kingly Priesthood and glory. He allows us to enjoy a foretaste of that love which makes us entirely one with Him, and which will live for ever in our hearts. Then our first and last thought about Jesus will be: Him who loved us.

IV. To Him be the Glory and Power for Ever and Ever.

The words of this song of praise are generally applied to God, but our Lord Jesus Christ is God, and they belong to Him also. He is worshipped here as our Redeemer. Now at the end of our series of meditations on His blood, and what He has obtained for us by that blood, these words of praise are a suitable expression for the feelings which ought to be ours—To Him be glory and power for ever and ever. These words came from a heart full of the joy of a personal experience of redemption. John writes as one who was living in the full enjoyment of the love of His Lord, and who knew and felt in his heart that he was cleansed in the blood; who experienced that Jesus had made him a King and a Priest. His thanksgiving is that of one who rejoices with "a joy unspeakable and full of glory"—a joy kindled by the song of heaven to which he had been listening. Let us lay this to our heart. Nothing will fit us for taking a real share in this thanksgiving which was offered involuntarily from the depth of a joyful heart, save a living experience of the love of Jesus, and of the power of His blood to cleanse us, and of the Kingly Priesthood in which He enables us to live. If I would truly attribute glory and power to Jesus, my heart must be inwardly filled with that glory and power. "Out of the abundance of the heart the mouth speaketh." Think of how true this was on the day of Pentecost. What was it moved a band of one hundred and twenty to praise and glorify the Lord? The Holy Spirit, who is the glory and power of the Lord Jesus, had descended upon them; and because they were filled with that glory and power their hearts could ascend in praise to Him, and from them streamed out blessings for others.

It is the glory and power of Jesus to bestow His love on a soul, and to effect its cleansing in His own blood, and to appoint such a one to His Kingly Priesthood. Then the heart overflows spontaneously—"To Him be glory and power for ever."

You who have accompanied us through God's Word to discover what the glory and power of the blood of Jesus is— ought not your lives and walk every day to be full of the notes of praise and worship—"To Him be the glory and power?"

This is possible. Jesus Himself is the centre of this three-fold blessing—the Love; the Blood; and the Kingly Priesthood. Jesus Himself will so reveal them to us by His Spirit that we shall ceaselessly experience all these blessings.

Let us, as far as our knowledge goes, at every remembrance of His love cry out : " To Him be the glory." Each time we are convicted that the praise we offer is too weak and too seldom heard, and that it has too little of the joy-note of heaven in it, may be a help to us, if it drives us to seek after such a fullness of blessing as shall make our hearts overflow.

Yes, it is possible. Jesus lives, and Jesus has loved us, and has Himself cleansed us in His blood. He bestows upon us the disposition of kingship and priesthood by His indwelling.

It is possible. He can fill our lives with the experience which finds expression in the thanksgiving : " To Him be the glory and power."

My brethren, we hope to meet one day amid that multitude who have washed their robes in the blood of the Lamb, and who never weary in singing : " Thou art worthy, for Thou hast purchased us to God by Thy blood." Let our exercises of preparation for that glory consist in the singing of that song : " To Him who loved us, and washed us from our sins in His own blood, and hath made us kings and priests to God and His Father, to Him be the glory for ever, Amen."